VICTORIAN
Britain & Ireland
IN COLOUR

THIS IS A SEVENOAKS BOOK

Photographs © Galerie Bilderwelt 2005
A World in Colour Introduction © Galerie Bilderwelt 2005
All other text and design © Carlton Books Limited 2005

This edition published in 2005 by Sevenoaks
An imprint of the Carlton Publishing Group
20 Mortimer Street
London
W1T 3JW

A CIP catalogue for this book is available from the British Library.

ISBN: 1 86200 211 8

Printed in Dubai

Executive Editor: Stella Caldwell
Design: Emma Wicks & Michelle Pickering
Production: Lisa Moore

VICTORIAN
Britain & Ireland
IN COLOUR

**JANICE ANDERSON
&
REINHARD SCHULTZ**

SevenOaks

CONTENTS

INTRODUCTION

The charmingly coloured pictures in this book offer a very attractive view of the British Isles in the Victorian Age. Here is a land of peaceful, even idyllic rural life and of spectacular scenery among mountains and lakes inland and wild cliffs and rocky foreshores on the coasts. It is a land where happy, relaxed crowds stroll along esplanades and piers at Blackpool and Brighton, Scarborough and Llandudno. And it is a land of delightfully unspoilt villages and towns, many dominated by a castle or two that were once essential for protection but which now provide picturesque ruins to attract visitors.

This attractive view, while a perfectly true and realistic picture of Britain and Ireland in the later 19th century, is not the whole truth. It cannot explain that these scenes are set in a British Isles where almost every aspect of life for a rapidly growing population was affected by the great flowering of science and invention that made the Industrial Revolution possible.

Of all the inventions of the Industrial Revolution, the steam-powered railway system had the greatest effect on life in Britain. The rapidly growing railway network allowed ordinary people to travel in unprecedented numbers. Time and again, as you read here about resorts in all four countries of the British Isles, you will discover that, without the railway, they would not have existed or, at least, would not have grown beyond the small fishing harbour or port that they had been for generations.

The railways, really getting into their stride in the 1830s, the decade in which the 18-year-old Victoria became Queen of Britain and Ireland, were soon reaching to all parts of the British Isles. As trains cost much less to travel in than horse-drawn coaches, by mid-century even poor rural farmworkers and villagers found they could afford a ticket to their nearest market town.

By this time, Mr Thomas Cook, a publisher and Temperance reformer from Market Harborough in

Leicestershire, had shown them that they could also use trains for excursions. Cook's first excursion, an outing for his local Temperance Association in July 1841, took 570 passengers, all with one shilling (5p) return tickets, on a day trip by a special excursion train hired from the Midland Railway Company from Leicester to Loughborough. Soon Cook was organizing complete holidays, such as Leicester to Glasgow, by train and steamer, for one guinea (£1.05). Ten years later, he was taking thousands of people to London for the Great Exhibition and within a couple of years had his first London office, first in Fleet Street then in Ludgate Circus. Mass excursion and holiday travel had begun.

While the better-off could travel, either independently or with Mr Cook, without worrying about the cost, for the factory workers of Britain's industrial cities things were not so easy early in Victoria's reign. As the century progressed, however, wages improved and – just as important – workers began to get more days off. Factory workers in Lancashire and Yorkshire had their Wakes Weeks, which took thousands to resorts like Blackpool in the autumn. Then the Bank Holidays Act of 1871 added four public holidays to the two (Good Friday and Christmas Day) that had been the custom throughout the century.

With time and wages that allowed them to buy tickets and rooms in hotels or boarding houses, the great mass of the people of Britain and Ireland could discover their own countries with an ease their grandparents could only have dreamed of. Many of the places that they visited in their thousands are depicted in this book.

JANICE ANDERSON

OPPOSITE LEFT: *The promenade in the coastal town of Deal, in the "Garden of England", the county of Kent.*
OPPOSITE RIGHT: *A view from Great Orme's Head, at Llandudno, Wales.*
BELOW LEFT: *A majestic-looking Dunottar Castle, at Stonehaven, Scotland*
BELOW RIGHT: *The harbour at Glengarriff in the county of Cork, in Ireland*

A WORLD IN COLOUR:
THE PHOTOCHROMS WE ONCE KNEW

In the Spring of 1896 groups of people gathered in front of the grandiose building in Ludgate Circus where Thomas Cook & Son had set up their agency, selling excursions to Luxor to the rich as well as more affordable travel abroad to the the rising middle classes of industrial Britain.

But it was not the announcement of the latest trip on a Nile paddle-steamer that kept people in an excited mood amongst the busy horse traffic, but the presentation of large-size scenic colour photos – as reported in the *Morris Trade Journal* – which had never been shown in a shop-window display in the city of London. A similar response was reported four years later when the so-called photochroms were presented at the *Exposition Universel* in Paris.

Here it was, finally, a new vision of far-away and exotic places people loved to visit. And the images were aimed right at this segment of the public that wanted to "follow the wonderful man from Cooks" as a song put it two years later. With the ancient barriers of time and space breached by railroads and steamships, the tour

BELOW: *The Station Hotel in Ayr, in Scotland. Many hotels sprang up next to railway stations to accommodate the increasing number of travellers who took advantage of the new transport system.*

round the empire was on the agenda, as was the souvenir picture to prove it and aid reminiscences.

In 1888, the Swiss company Orell Füssli & Co had patented the secret behind the new type of colour photos, which came to be known as photochroms. The actual inventor, who, of course, was never mentioned in this context, was the lithographer Hans Jakob Schmid who had worked for Füssli in Zurich since 1876. Schmid had experimented with asphalt lithography, which had already been applied by Viennese lithographers, who created the first photolithographic colour print in 1866. This was more than 30 years after Joseph Nicéphore Niépce had successfully tested bitumen of Judea (*asphaltum syricum*) on its response to light.

With a special formula coating on the limestone used in lithographic printing, Schmid was able to transfer half-tone negatives to the light-sensitive surface of the stone – one of which was used for each colour.

In the early years a small edition of 150–200 high quality lithographic prints was made using as many as six stones, but a few years later up to 18 rendered editions that often ran into the thousands. As a final treatment, the prints were coated with varnish, which added depth and a certain patina.

The mass production of the Swiss photochroms was eventually dominated by the Photoglob Co, which in

1895, was also based in Zurich, while agencies trading in the pictures had been set up in Detroit and London.

Three years later, the collections of images – taken by photographers about whom we know very little – consisted of more than 3.000 European scenic views.

Soon thousands more were added from Russia, Turkey, Syria, Palestine, Northern Africa and India, as well as the United States of America. Finally, Central and South America followed, as did Persia (now Iran), China, New South Wales in Australia and New Zealand. To promote the more than 14.000 prints available, the bilingual (German-French) *Bulletin Photoglob* was published until 1906 and advertised seven formats up to 42 x 90 cm (16 x 36 in). Photochroms were available with different finishes and passepartout frames in various colours and some were available on sheet metal as well as glass.

In 1896, Paul Felix Wild of the Photoglob Company

ABOVE: *A delightful view of the Pantiles, one of the oldest parts of Tunbridge Wells, once best known for its spa, where the Photochrom Company once had offices.*

sold exclusive American rights to the Detroit Publishing Company, one of the major art publishers and distributors in the world. In Britain, rights were granted to the Photochrom Company Ltd which had offices in London and Tunbridge Wells, in Kent. These companies shared the secrets of the *asphaltum syricum* surface which rendered the most beautiful colours known in printing at the time – and they worked hard to prevent competitors from finding out any of the details.

Despite the size of the international market and the millions of prints sold, the photochrom story somehow got lost along the way to our digital world. Its rediscovery was prompted in 1974, when someone "found" 11.000 vintage photochroms in the basement of the Zentralbibliothek (Central Library) in Zürich. But a comprehensive history and analysis of the impact of these colour images still remains to be written and the difficulty in trying to find a complete set of "Tuck's Gigantic Post Cards", such as the London Railway Stations (The Photochrome Series 9384), "beautifully reproduced in the latest Photo-Colour process ...", shows just how hard it would be.

Today, one might find fault with the colouring of the skies, rivers and sea. One might even question the tones of certain buildings, but given that one is assaulted by a wave of colour just walking down the street nowadays, one cannot escape the peculiar charm inherent in the softness of the photochroms. With their golden lettering they have turned into sacred incunabula of those days long gone, the *fin de siècle* which seems to be so innocent, magnificent and glorious but probably wasn't.

"The colour of London is the Glory of London. It has appealed to artists of every nationality, and even those from lands where colour riots under cloudless skies," wrote George R Sims in his introduction to the book *Fifty Colour Photographs Of London Reproduced by an Exclusive Process with Short Descriptions*. This rather rare book was published in London by the Photochrom Company, around 1912 and contains 50 captioned, tipped-in, colour plates with views of famous sites as well as of a City Policeman, the Postman, an Orderly Boy and a Flower Girl.

"And amid the modern mélange of colours that has transformed grim old London into a beautiful city, the quaint colour note of a bygone day still remains... For he who knows not the colour of London knows not the living London of today, but only the ghost of a London that is dead."

So somehow we really are not so far apart from where Mr Sims stood to view things almost a century ago.

REINHARD SCHULTZ
GALERIE BILDERWELT

ABOVE: *Carriages wait for visitors at the entrance to the castle in Conwy, in Wales. The mellow tones of the brickwork and the shadows falling on the stones are very true to life in this photocrom.*

BELOW: *The glory of the Tower of London is somewhat enhanced by the colour definition of this polychrom, which shows one of the country's most historic monuments from a view across the river Thames.*

CHAPTER ONE

LONDON
& ITS ENVIRONS

In 19th-century Britain, London's status was unique. It was the administrative and commercial capital of Great Britain and of the world's largest empire. The Roman port of Londinium had grown over the centuries, encompassing many villages north and south of the Thames, and was the largest city and port in the British Empire. Much of this power and grandeur was reflected in the building works of the Victorian Age. True, the Tower of London had been built 1000 years before, and many other buildings also dated back centuries, but the Victorians left their mark everywhere, in great technical achievements like Tower Bridge and the Holborn Viaduct and in the glasshouses that sheltered the great botanic collections of Kew Gardens.

ABOVE: *The Thames downstream from Hungerford Bridge, with a paddle steamer taking on passengers at Charing Cross Pier, and Cleopatra's Needle, brought to England from Eygpt in 1878, reaching up from its sphinx-guarded base on the Embankment.*

RIGHT: *Londoners stroll through the archway at Horse Guards, headquarters of the Household Cavalry, into Whitehall. Horse Guards and the uniforms of its mounted troopers have changed little since it was built in the mid-18th century.*

RIGHT: *A Yeoman Warder of the Tower of London, stands proudly to attention in his gorgeous Tudor uniform. Dating from the 11th century, when William the Conqueror began its construction, the Tower of London has been a fortress, a royal palace and a prison, housing royal and commoner prisoners. For Victorians, including Gilbert and Sullivan, whose* The Yeoman of the Guard, *was an immensely popular operetta, the Tower was a must-see attraction.*

BELOW: *The 1000-ton bascules of Tower Bridge are raised to allow a paddle steamer through into the Pool of London. Tower Bridge was built between 1881 and 1894 in a Gothic style, chosen to harmonize with the architecture of the Tower of London (to the right). The Gothic stonework hides some very high-tech Victorian steel construction. The bascules could be raised so quickly that the footbridge put on top to allow uninterrupted pedestrian traffic was not needed.*

BELOW: *The turreted and crenellated White Tower dominates the cluster of buildings that make up the Tower of London. The White Tower was built to the orders of William the Conqueror, and got its name nearly two centuries later when Henry III, who lived there, had its exterior white-washed. Visitors late in Victoria's reign could see the Tower's splendid armouries and the Crown jewels but not the caged animals, for the Tower's Royal Menagerie had been closed.*

ABOVE: *Business of all kinds takes crowds of people, in carriages, cabs and waggons and on foot over London Bridge to and from the City. For many centuries, the wooden London Bridge, one of the wonders of medieval Europe, was the city's only bridge and a street in itself with shops and houses. It was replaced, between 1823 and 1831, by this elegant granite bridge, designed by the Scottish engineer, John Rennie.*

OPPOSITE: *Cheapside was an important thoroughfare in London in late Roman times and did not lose its importance in the centuries that followed. Here, the street is busy with its usual weekday traffic. Bank clerks and businessmen, ladies and gentlemen out shopping, a policeman and a milkman, all crowd the pavements or dodge the open-topped omnibuses, delivery vans and waggons that fill the roadway.*

ABOVE: *Beyond Cheapside to the East was Bank, the commercial centre of the City of London. Here, behind a blind security wall, was the Bank of England (on the left) and, on the right, the classically-colonnaded Royal Exchange, with an equestrian statue of the Duke of Wellington in front. The Royal Exchange was founded in Elizabeth I's reign, and the Bank of England not until 1694, but it was the latter that quickly came to dominate Britain's financial life.*

LEFT: *The 100-bed Great Western Hotel, was the largest hotel in England when it opened next to Paddington Station. The station was built in 1850-4, 15 years after Isambard Kingdom Brunel began building the Great Western Railway. The GWR – known to many of those who built it, worked for it and travelled on it as God's Wonderful Railway – took travellers from Paddington to Bristol and on to Wales.*

BELOW: *The British Museum came to epitomise for Victorians all that was finest in learning and scholarship. The museum was established in the mid-18th century to house several private collections and the Royal Library. It grew rapidly and in 1823 moved into a new building in Bloomsbury, designed in the Classical style by Sir Robert Smirke. It was not completed until 1847, the tenth year of Victoria's reign.*

ABOVE: *The splendid Messrs Burroughs Wellcome and Co. factory at Dartford, in east London. Silas Burroughs and Henry Wellcome were representatives of US drug companies in England who grasped the opportunity of the British-led revolution in mass drug production to found their own pharmaceutical company in London in 1880. By the turn of the century their company had a big international network.*

RIGHT: *Holborn, once a village on the outskirts of London, was, by Victoria's reign, a busy commercial area of London, with many law firms. The Holborn Viaduct, the world's first "fly-over", was built in the 1860s to bridge the valley of the old Fleet river (now flowing underground). The Viaduct linked Cheapside and Oxford Street, creating a good through route, but meant the demolition of thousands of slum dwellings.*

ABOVE: *Admiral Lord Nelson, victor of the Battle of Trafalgar in 1805, gazes down Whitehall from his vantage point 185 feet (56m) above Trafalgar Square. The square was laid out in the 1830s to commemorate the great naval victory. Nelson's Column, with its three-times lifesize statue of Nelson on top, was built in 1843. The four great bronze lions that guard it were designed by Sir Edwin Landseer, famous for his fine, but often sentimental, animal paintings.*

RIGHT: *Piccadilly Circus in the 1890s, watched over by London's first aluminium statue. The winged archer was intended by its creator, Sir Alfred Gilbert, to be the Angel of Christian Charity, but very quickly after its unveiling in 1893 it was dubbed "Eros". There is not yet an Underground line rumbling under the Circus, and the public transport consists of omnibuses, using the pavement round Eros as a stopping point, and hackney cabs.*

RIGHT: *Rather grubby with the soot from London's chimneys, but still magnificently imposing, St Paul's Cathedral and its great dome dominate Ludgate Hill, one of the two highest points in the City of London. The finest work of Sir Christopher Wren, the cathedral replaced "Old St Paul's", which was destroyed in the Great Fire of London in 1666. St Paul's was completed in the reign of Queen Anne, whose statue stands before the cathedral's West Front.*

BELOW: *Westminster Abbey has a special status among English churches. It is a "Royal Peculiar", which means it does not come under the jurisdiction of a bishop. This results from the fact that the Abbey, or the Collegiate Church of St Peter at Westminster, to give it its full name, has been the place of coronation for every English sovereign, except Edward V and Edward VIII, since 1066. It is also the burial place of kings, queens, poets and great men and women.*

BELOW: *Take away the horse-drawn traffic and the sand on the roadway (put down to make sweeping up horse droppings easier) and this view of the Houses of Parliament and Westminster Bridge could have been made a hundred years later. Of course, for Queen Victoria and her older subjects, the Parliament buildings were still a novelty. The old Palace of Westminster was destroyed in a massive fire in 1834 and the buildings that replaced it took 25 years to complete.*

ABOVE: *Hyde Park Corner in the 1890s. It already has traffic islands to help direct the flow of traffic and to give pedestrians necessary refuges in mid-roadway. There is no sign of the iron shutters that the Duke of Wellington had to erect on his town house, Apsley House (to the right of the arched gateways into Hyde Park) during the parliamentary reform riots of 1831. It was the shutters, rather than his military exploits, which included winning the Battle of Waterloo, that got Wellington his "Iron Duke" nickname.*

RIGHT: *The parks of London had long been one of the city's greatest glories, people frequenting them for exercise and for socialising. The largest of them, Hyde Park, was once Henry VIII's hunting ground and Charles II opened it to the public. Hyde Park, and its mile-long riding path, Rotten Row, with its paths for walkers on either side, were especially fashionable throughout the 19th century. Anyone doing the London Season had to be seen strolling or riding there regularly, especially after church on Sunday mornings.*

LEFT: *Queen Victoria was still very much alive when this gloriously over-the-top memorial to her dead husband, Prince Albert, the Prince Consort, was built in Hyde Park in 1876, so any adverse comments on its artistic merits were muted. In fact, the Albert Memorial was well-deserved and it is appropriate that the Prince's statue should face in the direction of the great museums of South Kensington that he did so much to make possible.*

BELOW: *Kensington Gardens, a westwards extension of Hyde Park, were the grounds of a private residence until William of Orange converted the house into a palace. Queen Victoria was born in Kensington Palace and lived there until shortly after her accession. While the palace was neglected for much of the 19th century, the gardens were not, and these grand fountains, on the northern side of the gardens, provided Victorians with an elegant setting for a Sunday stroll.*

ABOVE: *The Royal Botanic Gardens at Kew, in the grounds of a former royal palace and private botanic garden, were one of the finest practical expressions of the Victorians' deep interest in horticulture and botany. The nation's main scientific depository for plant species and varieties from all over the world, Kew Gardens were opened to the public in 1841. As well as acres of gardens, Kew had a museum, set by a lake and splendid glasshouses.*

ABOVE: *On the Thames in Surrey, Richmond in Victoria's reign was in reality an affluent suburb of London, a fact emphasized by the arrival of a branch of the London Underground's District Line in 1877. Because it was an easy trip by royal barge downriver to London, Richmond had been a favoured place with the Tudor monarchs. Elizabeth I, indomitable to the last, died at Richmond Palace, sitting upright on a cushion rather than lying in her bed.*

RIGHT: *Windsor Castle, set on a chalk bluff above the Thames in Berkshire. The castle was a favourite out-of-London home for Queen Victoria and Prince Albert, especially after the railway reached the royal borough and made getting there so quick and easy. The Queen's grandfather, George III, and uncle, George IV, had done much to restore the Castle to its former grandeur, and Victoria contented herself with building the Royal Mausoleum at Frogmore.*

OPPOSITE: *The formal gardens on Windsor Castle's East Terrace show how far the castle had moved away from its original defensive purpose to becoming a family home – albeit a very grand one. From the East Terrace, Victoria and Albert had an excellent view of the Home Park and its private gardens beneath the castle ramparts, and of the Great Park, the remains of the vast royal hunting forest of the medieval kings, beyond it.*

ABOVE: *The Victorians loved messing about in boats, especially if the messing about could be done at such a fashionable place as Boulter's Lock on the Thames at Maidenhead. This crowded scene could be taking place at a Bank Holiday weekend. Or it could be the Sunday after Royal Ascot in June, a particularly fashionable day to be seen in a skiff or punt (probably hired), dressed in one's most up-to-the-minute clothes.*

CHAPTER TWO

SOUTH-EAST ENGLAND

England's south-east corner, jutting out into the English Channel towards the Continent (so near that it could be seen from the White Cliffs of Dover), was the richest and most densely populated part of Victorian Britain. The Railway Age, beginning a few years before Victoria's accession in 1837, brought most of the region much closer to London. Within a few decades it was possible to live in many of its attractive towns, including those on the River Thames and along the coasts, while earning a living in London. As the large number of pictures of them here indicate, the South-east's coastal towns benefited greatly from the coming of the railway.

ABOVE: *Behind the Georgian fronts of the buildings along High Street in Guildford, the county town of Surrey, lie many much older buildings. The Guildhall, whose clock projects out over the street, has a Tudor building behind its 17th-century façade.*

RIGHT: *George, Prince of Wales, visited Brighton in 1783, and the Sussex seaside town never looked back. A century later, the railway was bringing in thousands of holiday-makers to enjoy Brighton's beach, piers, amusements arcades and aquarium.*

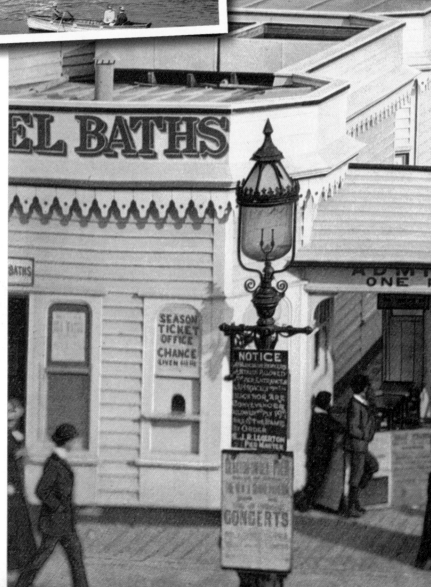

ABOVE: *Southend, a small fishing town on the north side of the Thames Estuary, was very popular with Londoners, partly because it could be reached by train in little more than an hour from Liverpool Street Station. This view of the West Parade promenade and boat jetty could be enjoyed by everyone strolling along Southend pier, which, at a mile and a quarter, was the longest in Great Britain. There was no need to walk it, however; an electric tramway took people from the top to the pier head in five minutes.*

RIGHT: *The entrance to the pier at Clacton-on-Sea, on the Essex coast. A strong sea wall with a promenade behind it and several openings down on to the sandy, safe-for-bathing beach, and the pier, both built in the 1880s, led to Clacton-on-Sea's rapid rise in popularity from then on. The town had a fine lifeboat station, built with funds given to the Royal National Lifeboat Institution by the Prince of Wales. Naturally, Clacton's first lifeboat, which had a 15-man crew, was named Albert Edward.*

LEFT: *The great keep of Rochester Castle, a fine example of Norman military building, towers over the port and cathedral city of Rochester, on the lower reaches of the River Medway in Kent. The peaceful park, laid out in the castle's bailey, has benches ideally placed for girls to take a rest from bowling hoops or nannies from pushing babies in perambulators. Charles Dickens must have liked Rochester, for the city featured many times in his books.*

BELOW: *Chatham, on the Medway in Kent, has long been a naval town. Elizabeth I ordered the building of Chatham Dockyard, and later monarchs expanded it. Nelson's flagship, Victory, was built at Chatham and Charles Dickens's father, John, worked in the Navy Pay Office here. Dickens described Chatham in* Pickwick Papers *as noisy, smelly, dirty and littered with drunks. To judge from this tranquil scene, Chatham was much changed later in the century.*

ABOVE: *Canterbury's beginnings can be traced back to the Iron Age, but it was the Romans who first saw the strategic value of the trading settlement in Kent. The town's Westgate, standing some way from the great cathedral, was built in the 14th century as a fortified gate into the city. Victorians, not much bothered by the fact that it had been used as a prison for many years, climbed to the top of Westgate for its magnificent views over the city's roofs to the cathedral.*

ABOVE: *The busy High Street of Maidstone, the county town of Kent. Maidstone's position in the heart of the agriculturally-rich county ensured it a big role as a market town from the Middle Ages. By Victorian times, however, Maidstone's famous linen thread-making industry had declined, and many of the flax fields were turned over to hops for the brewing industry. The town's old water-driven textile mills were still in use, but were now making paper.*

RIGHT: *Herne Bay, near Reculver on the Kent coast facing the German Ocean, as the Victorians called the North Sea, did not greatly appeal to holiday-makers until a branch of the London, Chatham and Dover Railway reached there in 1862. Even then, it remained a quietly middle-class sort of place, quite different from noisy Margate and Ramsgate. Herne Bay had a fine pier, built by the Thomas Telford in 1832. It reached more than 3000 feet out into the bracing air of the German Ocean.*

BELOW: *On its marine parade, Herne Bay boasted a splendid colonnaded clock tower, the gift of a "private lady", who provided the £4000 the clock cost. Much of the town's social life went on round it, including the selling of souvenirs and ice creams. At the seaside, ice cream could be bought in "penny licks" – that is, a penny's-worth of ice cream in a shallow glass that was returned to the stall-holder when the ice cream had been eaten.*

ABOVE: *Children stop for the photographer under the York Gate arch at Broadstairs. This quiet seaside town on the Thanet coast of Kent was seen by many Victorians as being more genteel and select than its larger and more noisy neighbours, Ramsgate and Margate. Charles Dickens had liked Broadstairs and lived in a house which, now called "Bleak House", was still in the 1890s pointed out to visitors as the chief monument of the town.*

ABOVE: *The cliff-top town of Margate, on the north-facing coast of the Isle of Thanet in Kent, became a popular watering-place for Londoners early in the 19th century, when steamers began taking trippers downriver to the former fishing port. Then came the railways, and Margate blossomed hugely. In mid-century, the jetty and harbour were extended and enlarged, and provided with a grand hexagonal promenade which doubled as a landing stage for steamers and yachts.*

OPPOSITE: *Ignoring the chance to hire a donkey to take them down, holiday-makers in Margate make their way down The Gap, one of many ways down from Margate's cliff-top setting to the sands. Others stand on the footbridge over The Gap, taking in the splendid view of the crowded sands. A few of Margate's many bathing machines can be seen drawn out to sea in the distance. As Margate faced north, it was more windy and less sunny than its rival, Ramsgate.*

RIGHT: *The beach and ladies' bathing place at Margate. By the late Victorian age, not all women felt it necessary to slip into the sea from behind the modesty curtain erected over the steps of their bathing machine, especially if there was a section of beach set aside just for them. Bathing machines were rather dark and dank and although, as this picture shows, they were still on the beach in great numbers, many younger women and girls were choosing not to use them.*

LEFT: *Follies, such as this carefully contrived waterfall, were among the many attractions created for visitors to Ramsgate, the Isle of Thanet's hugely popular seaside resort. Ramsgate's career as a watering-place began in the mid-18th century, when the harbour and a new pier were built. Steamships ran regular services from London to Ramsgate early in the 19th century, and when the railway arrived, to a station built right by the crowded sands, Ramsgate's continuing popularity as a seaside resort was assured.*

BELOW: *Ramsgate Sands crammed into their relatively small area everything visitors needed to enjoy their time at the seaside. Beach entertainers, donkeys, Punch and Judy stands, photographers and print sellers, trinket sellers, boatmen and bathing machine attendants fought to attract the attention of men and women, many of whom sat on ordinary kitchen and dining chairs at the water's edge reading books.*

RIGHT: *New Road, with a promenade above it, ran by Ramsgate's harbour, to which George IV had given the style "Royal" in 1821. Its grand style indicates just how superior the town thought itself to its more vulgar neighbour, Margate. As an 1895 guide to Britain's coastal towns put it, "We find here large numbers of really fine private houses. Some of the public buildings, too, are decidedly superior in style."*

LEFT: *The huge bulk of Dover Castle, one of England's greatest fortifications, stands proudly on its hill overlooking the public gardens of Dover, England's premier Channel port. A favourite walk for visitors to Dover was along the top of Shakespeare's Cliff, from where on clear days there were wide-ranging views of the coast of France. A branch of the South-Eastern Railway to Folkestone ran through a tunnel under the white chalk cliff.*

ABOVE: *Although Dover was a port rather than a resort, it did cater for visitors, who came to the town in summer by train and by steamboats from London. Pulley systems, rather than horses, were used to pull bathing machines on the small beach in and out of the water. Until 1890, when it closed, Crabble Mill, a working flour mill, could be visited. The mill was built in 1812 to provide flour for troops stationed in Dover Castle during the Napoleonic Wars.*

LEFT: *The tall fishing net drying huts and the fishing boats drawn up on the beach below the East Cliff at Hastings, in Sussex, emphasize the importance of the fishing industry here. Hastings's fish market operated from a site by the drying huts. The occasional "Dutch" fish auctions, when the fish seller would name his price, then steadily decrease it, by sixpence or so each time, until he had a buyer were an extra attraction for visitors.*

OPPOSITE: *Yachts taking holiday-makers on sea trips leave from a jetty on the beach at Hastings. The town went to considerable expense in the later 19th century to cater for visitors, especially in the matter of sea-bathing. Fine baths, including a separate swimming bath, were built under the sea-front parade near the pier in 1879 at a cost of £62,000 – twice what it had cost to build the pier, which included a pavilion large enough to seat 2000 people.*

ABOVE: *All is peace and quiet in the High Street of Battle, the Sussex town inland from Hastings where the Battle of Hastings was actually fought in 1066. Goods are being unloaded from a waggon in front of the Abbey Hotel, no doubt named after the abbey that William the Conqueror built on the hilltop where Harold, leader of the English, was killed. St Martin's Abbey was consecrated in 1094 and was dissolved in the 16th century by Henry VIII.*

ABOVE: *Penshurst Place, near Tunbridge Wells in Kent, was given to Sir William Sidney, uncle of the poet Sir Philip Sidney, in the 16th century. Much careful reconstruction, especially of the house's stone walls and towers, was undertaken by the Sidney family in Victorian times and fine formal gardens were laid out in the 1850s. It is not surprising, then, that Penshurst Place was high on the Victorians' list of historic houses to be visited on open days.*

OPPOSITE: *The Pantiles, an elegant colonnaded shopping street in the Kent spa town of Royal Tunbridge Wells, got its name from the baked tiles that were laid on the pavement when the street was first built in the early 18th century. By the late 19th century, the Pantiles was little changed, remaining one of the most elegant shopping streets in England, but most of the pantiles had gone, having been replaced by much more hard-wearing Purbeck flagstones.*

ABOVE: *The Victorians called Brighton "The Queen of Watering Places". There was no place in England to rival the great Sussex seaside town, presenting, as it did, "such a façade to the sea as probably no other watering-place in the world can rival," to quote an 1890s guide book. When Dr Russell of Brighton wrote his treatise on the benefits of sea-bathing in the 18th century, the place was a small fishing village. A century later hotels the size of the 600-bed Metropole (above) were accommodating visitors.*

RIGHT: *Brighton's Aquarium did much more than simply cater to the Victorian interest in seashells, seaweed and other marine life. A joint stock company was formed to erect the extremely costly building, which opened in 1872. Its 41 fish tanks were supplied with sea water from huge reservoirs into which the water was pumped by steam. Visitors tiring of looking at fish and other marine life, could converse in a conservatory, or read newspapers, periodicals and "the latest telegrams" in several elegant saloons.*

LEFT: *The pier at Worthing. On the Sussex coast west of Brighton, Worthing was considered early in the 19th century to be much more genteel than its neighbour. Later, it added to its attractions a pier and a splendid esplanade, from which the lights of Brighton could be seen at night. Then came disaster when its water supply was tainted and typhoid stalked the town. By the 1890s, its water supply was above reproach and visitors had returned to its smooth sands.*

OPPOSITE: *Worthing's South Street, leading up through the town from the Marine Parade to the Town Hall. A quietly attractive watering-place, Worthing in the late 19th century was also a major provider of fruit and vegetables to Covent Garden market in London. Fifteen miles of local glasshouses grew grapes, figs, tomatoes and other mild-climate produce. Much less appreciated was the strong-smelling seaweed that piled up on the sands in winter.*

BELOW: *Littlehampton, lying between Worthing and Bognor on the Sussex coast, could not boast a pleasure pier, but its jetty alongside the harbour was often boosted to the status of one, at least on postcards. The small, quiet resort was considered ideal for children, the broad, flat sands being perfectly safe, with no stones or rock pools for small toes to be stubbed against. Bored older children could take a boat trip up the River Arun to Arundel Castle.*

RIGHT: *The sands and East Parade at Bognor in the 1890s. By this time, Bognor had a sea wall, a fine esplanade and a lengthy pier, all paid for by the Local Board in an effort to increase the town's numbers of holiday-makers. Most of the bathing machines have been pulled down to the water's edge, rather than right into it; by this time they were being used more as changing cabins than as places from which modest women could slip unobserved into the sea.*

BELOW: *The New East Parade at Bognor. In 1785 a wealthy London hatter, Sir Richard Hotham, discovered quiet, mild-weathered Bognor at the western end of Sussex. He spent a fortune, building commodious villas and the like, in an attempt to make Bognor a "truly recherché" watering-place. He failed and through the 19th century Bognor remained quiet, with Sir Richard remembered only in the name of one of Bognor's best streets, Hotham Place.*

RIGHT: *Rough seas at Bognor, with the hotel in the centre of the picture above almost disappearing behind the sea spray. Seaside resorts in Britain at the turn of the century made sure they had a few "Rough Seas At…" postcards on sale. They added greatly to the Victorian's romantic vision of the sea as something thrillingly dangerous and awe-inspiring. The same romantic notion sent holiday-makers walking to the end of the pier, far out to sea.*

CHAPTER THREE

WESSEX

At the beginning of the Victorian Age, in that part of England known as Wessex (traditionally encompassing Hampshire, Wiltshire, Dorset and Somerset, with parts of Devon, Gloucestershire, Oxfordshire and Berkshire sometimes added), traditional rural communities and values had been relatively untouched by the Industrial Revolution. By the time of Victoria's death in 1901, life in Wessex had changed radically. The Wessex illustrated in these pages is not far removed from the novels of Thomas Hardy. He used the real region and a fictionalized version of it as the setting for stories that combined personal dramas with deeply felt descriptions of the impact of the changes during Victoria's reign that most affected the lives of rural people.

LEFT: *For Victorians, Southsea was unique among watering-places. Lying at the western end of the great naval base, Portsmouth, its life was all bands and reviews on land and a constant movement of yachts, steamers and battleships out on the Solent.*

ABOVE: *The tower of Magdalen College rising above Magdalen Bridge across the Cherwell, made up the first view of Oxford University for many visitors to the city. Beyond lay the High, with most of the ancient university's colleges on or near it.*

ABOVE: *The tree-lined avenue up to the great West Door of Winchester Cathedral, as familiar a walk to late Victorians as it had been to Jane Austen and her family early in the 19th century. The city of Winchester, in Hampshire, was England's first capital city. The Normans began the building of the cathedral, on the site of a church built by the Saxon king, Alfred, in 1079. By the time it was completed, 300 years later, the cathedral was the longest in Europe and a magnificent example of Norman architecture.*

RIGHT: *Two eights preparing to race at Henley Royal Regatta. The market town of Henley-on-Thames (in Berkshire until the redrawing of country boundaries in the 20th century put in it Oxfordshire) was built along a mile-long straight stretch of the twisting River Thames, ideal for rowing. The first Henley regatta was held in 1839 and was given the title "Royal" by its patron, Prince Albert. The regatta, with its "garden party" air, quickly became a major event in the social life of middle-class Victorians.*

LEFT: *The Town Hall at Portsmouth, built in an imposing style befitting England's most important naval station. The Tudors set up the first royal dockyard here and Nelson, cheered by vast crowds, boarded HMS* Victory *here in 1805, sailing to immortality at Trafalgar. Isambard Kingdom Brunel was born here, as was Sherlock Holmes, the creation of a Portsmouth doctor, Arthur Conan Doyle.*

BELOW: *HMS* Victory *moored in Portsmouth Harbour. Victory was retired from service in 1824 and became the flagship of Portsmouth Command. Still a centre of naval social life, it was also a great tourist attraction. Every visitor was shown the spot where Nelson was mortally wounded and the corner in the cockpit where, as the guide books put it, "his indomitable spirit passed away".*

ABOVE: *The "peerless" Isle of Wight, across the Solent from Portsmouth, was very popular with Victorians, who spent summers at such delightful resorts as Shanklin (above). Queen Victoria and Prince Albert had a summer retreat, Osborne House, near the yachting centre of Cowes, and the Poet Laureate, Lord Tennyson, had a house called Farringford, near Freshwater.*

RIGHT: *Southsea, Portsmouth's beach suburb much favoured as a holiday residence by old naval officers, boasted a long esplanade, naturally enough adorned with some fine examples of naval ordnance, as well as the usual stalls of trinket, postcard and ice cream sellers. The beach here was shingly, and the Portsmouth Swimming Club had helped make sea-bathing more comfortable by building a bathing stage leading off the esplanade.*

LEFT: *The slim spire of Salisbury Cathedral soars above the river meadows surrounding Salisbury. The city, built at the meeting point of the valleys of four rivers that watered the Salisbury Plain, was planned in the 13th century by bishops who wanted a neat town around the cathedral they had founded in 1220. Building work was quick, and the cathedral, in the Early English Gothic style, was completed, except for the spire, within 60 years.*

OPPOSITE: *A view that inspired artists: Salisbury Cathedral seen from the water meadows surrounding Salisbury. The cathedral's magnificent spire, at 404 feet (123 metres) the tallest on an English cathedral, was added to the cathedral in the 14th century. Among the many artists inspired by the cathedral and its soaring spire, perhaps the greatest was John Constable.*

ABOVE: *Stonehenge, on the Salisbury Plain, as the Victorians knew it, with many of its massive stones lying on the earth where they had fallen centuries before. The mighty Druid monument held a strong fascination for the Victorians. From royalty to bank clerks, countesses to housemaids, they visited it in great numbers, picnicing in the shadow of the stones and photographing themselves walking around it and leaving the marks of their carriage wheels on the ground.*

ABOVE: *The entrance to the pier at Southampton. The Victorian Age knew Southampton, ideally situated on a deep and enclosed estuary on the Channel, as a thriving port, whose floating and dry docks could handle the largest ships of the world's largest merchant navy. But it was also a seaside resort, whose Royal Pier had been opened in 1832 by the Queen, when she was Princess Victoria, and which had a railway station, pavilion and promenade.*

OPPOSITE: *Southampton's West Gate, one of the gates built into the Norman fortifications of the city. West Gate confronted the West Quay, one of the oldest sections of the fortified town. In the 1890s, it had not been "too well preserved", so that it was still of "much interest", especially to visitors leaving the nearby club house of the Royal Southern Yacht Club.*

LEFT: *Dorchester, the county town of Dorset, seen from across the quiet meadowland around it. This ancient town, site of a Saxon mint in the 10th century, was the capital of Thomas Hardy's Wessex, featuring as Casterbridge in his novels. Hardy was born at Higher Bockhampton, just outside Dorchester, in 1840, and, after training as an architect, built a house called Max Gate in Dorchester.*

OPPOSITE: *The Borough Gardens in Dorchester. In developing their public gardens and providing them with plenty of seats and a bandstand, the town councillors of Dorchester were following a major trend in Victorian town planning. Throughout Britain, a great many parks and gardens, until now privately owned, were opened to the general public and new, beautifully landscaped parks were created, often paid for by public subscription.*

ABOVE: *High West Street in Dorchester, as Thomas Hardy knew it. Judge Jeffries lodged in the street while conducting his Bloody Assizes after the Monmouth Rebellion. And in the Old Crown Court in 1834, the six Tolpuddle Martyrs were sentenced to transportation after forming a Friendly Society – the beginnings of the trade-union movement in Britain. In Hardy's novels, Tolpuddle, a village near Dorchester, became Tolchurch.*

BELOW: *Sea-bathing in Britain was given the royal seal of approval at Weymouth, on the Dorset coast. In 1789, George III, on the advice of his doctors, chose Weymouth as the place for his, and the Royal Family's, first experiment with sea-bathing. As the royal head dipped below the waves, a band concealed in the next bathing machine struck up "God save Great George, our King". The king needed no saving and made annual visits to Weymouth for many years.*

LEFT: *The firm, smooth sands below the esplanade at Weymouth were ideal for children – and babies in perambulators. The splendid clock tower in the centre of the esplanade was erected to mark Queen Victoria's Jubilee in 1887. Since 1810, there had been a statue of George III further along the esplanade, put there to commemorate the 50th anniversary of the Accession of the town's greatest patron.*

BELOW: *Beach photographers, ice cream stalls, fish sellers and a Punch and Judy show cater for visitors thronging the sands at Weston-super-Mare. This west-of-England seaside resort grew in popularity, particularly with people from the Midlands, throughout the 19th century. Weston-super-Mare benefited greatly from being only 20 miles from Bristol, where the Great Western Railway first terminated.*

RIGHT: *The Market Cross at Cheddar, in the Mendip Hills. Famous for the cheese that originated here in the 17th century, Cheddar was of more interest to Victorians for its position at the foot of the famous Cheddar Gorge. The towering limestone cliffs of the Gorge were on many Victorians' must-see lists. Unfortunately, their favourite souvenir from the Gorge was the unique Cheddar Pink wild flower, which is why it is now a rarity.*

BELOW: *Fine stone buildings from pagan Rome and English Christianity next to each other in the West Country city of Bath. The warm mineral springs that led the Romans to build their superb baths there also attracted the fashionable folk of Georgian England. People came to Bath until well on into Victoria's reign to "take the waters" – even though, as Sam Weller remarked in* Pickwick Papers, *they tasted like "warm flat-irons".*

ABOVE: *Isambard Kingdom Brunel designed the magnificent Clifton Suspension Bridge spanning the Avon Gorge at Bristol. One of the great feats of Victorian engineering, the finished bridge incorporated 1,500 tons of British steel. Lack of funds meant that work on it was stopped when only the brick abutments had been built. The Institute of Civil Engineers finished it in 1864, five years after Brunel's death.*

RIGHT: *St Augustine's Bridge, Bristol. Built round a natural harbour on a river that flowed into the Severn Estuary, Bristol was a flourishing commercial port from as early as the 10th century. In the first years of Victoria's reign, it seemed as though Bristol would be playing a big part in the transatlantic trade, for Brunel built his two great steamships, the* Great Western *and the* Great Britain *here, but the trade moved to Liverpool.*

BELOW: *A view down Oxford's High Street, including many of the university's colleges. The ancient university city experienced enormous changes during the Victorian Age. The greatest debates over the theories of Charles Darwin took place there, and in 1870, when dons still had to be celibate, the university took the revolutionary step of opening examinations to women. Within a decade, women had their own hostels, which soon became full colleges.*

LEFT: *Oxford's Sheldonian Theatre was designed by Sir Christopher Wren in the style of a Roman theatre. It was named after its benefactor, Archbishop Sheldon, and was first used as a printing place for university books. By the 19th century, it had become a place for university functions and concerts.*

ABOVE: *The Oxford college, Christ Church, known as "the House". It was founded by Archbishop Wolsey during the reign of Henry VIII and when the Cardinal was disgraced, the college was renamed King Henry VIII's College. When the college's chapel also became the Oxford diocese's cathedral, the college was renamed again, this time Christ Church. Many scenes in Thomas Hardy's* Jude the Obscure *were set in Oxford (which Hardy called "Christminster") and Christ Church became "Cardinal College".*

CHAPTER FOUR

SOUTH-WEST ENGLAND

The two large counties of Devon and Cornwall, filling the great southern peninsula that thrusts out into the Atlantic Ocean, began to experience in the 19th century the process that, in the 20th, turned South-West England into Britain's most popular holiday region. The region already had the most mild and equable climate in Britain, some of its finest, wildest and most rugged scenery, and a wonderfully varied array of seaside resorts and many historic inland towns. All Victorians needed was an easy way of getting there. And the railway, aided by Isambard Kingdom Brunel's great railway bridge over the Tamar, opened in 1859, provided it.

ABOVE: *Collecting shells on Barricane Beach, near Morthoe, on Devon's north coast. The beach was famous for its shells, swept ashore by the incoming tide, and many were gathered up by local people to use in the making of seaside souvenirs.*

RIGHT: *The harbour at Brixham, Devon, one of the most important fishing stations on England's south coast. In the late 19th century some 200 fishing trawlers were based in Brixham and went out to the great Tor Bay fishery every day except Sunday.*

ABOVE: *Time for a chat in Exeter's High Street. Many buildings along the street were centuries old, for the Romans and the Saxons had both built settlements at Exeter and the cathedral city had long been the chief town in South-West England. In the first year of Victoria's reign, Charles Dickens found the model for his Fat Boy in* Pickwick Papers *working in the Turk's Head Inn in the High Street.*

OPPOSITE: *Lovers' Leap, another place of Dartmoor legend, this time at Holne Chase, near Holne, a village high above the valley of the River Dart. Charles Kingsley, author of* The Water Babies, *the great Victorian novel about the evils of child labour, was born at the old vicarage in Holne.*

RIGHT: *Legend has it that the church on top of Brent Tor on Dartmoor was built in the 12th century by a merchant wishing to show his gratitude to God for saving one of his ships from being wrecked. The legend would have appealed to Victorians, drawn to Dartmoor by its wild and rugged beauty and its romantic history.*

BELOW: *The village blacksmith with a customer – a horse ready
for shoeing – at Cockington, an attractive village of thatched
houses near Torquay. The forge, under its steeply sloping thatched
roof, had been in the centre of the village since the 14th century,
and the manor house at Cockington was Elizabethan.*

LEFT: *Bathing machines lined up on the sands at Teignmouth, on Babbacombe Bay. Early in the 19th century, Teignmouth began to grow beyond the small hamlet that had existed in Saxon times. First, came a quay, built in 1830, from which Dartmoor granite was shipped to London and used to build London Bridge. Then came the railway, which involved the considerable engineering feat of boring several tunnels through the cliffs along the coast here.*

ABOVE: *The broad, shallow beach at Paignton, south-west of Torquay on Tor Bay, ensured the fishing village's popularity as a watering-place – once the Great Western Railway had reached Torquay in 1848. Paignton owed its rapid growth in Victorian times to several entrepreneurs and industrialists, including Isaac Singer, of sewing-machine fame, who became patrons of the place, building fine hotels and villas to attract the middle classes.*

ABOVE: *The Royal Albert Bridge over the Tamar river linked Saltash and Plymouth. Designed by Isambard Kingdom Brunel, the railway bridge carried the Great Western Railway on from Devon into Cornwall. The bridge was opened by Prince Albert in 1859*

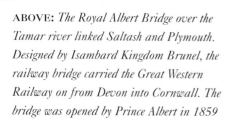

RIGHT: *The Eddystone Lighthouse, built on the Eddystone rocks, a great danger to shipping 14 miles (22.6km) off Plymouth. This lighthouse, the fifth to be built there, began its work in 1882. The lighthouse before it, John Smeaton's granite tower, was built in 1759 and guided shipping away from the rocks for 120 years. When cracks appeared in the rocks, not the lighthouse, it was dismantled and re-erected on Plymouth Hoe, opening to the public in 1884.*

BELOW: *The pleasure pier at Plymouth, with Drake's Island in the background. At the western extremity of Devon, Plymouth became an important port and naval base in the 16th century, not because Elizabeth I's government wished it so, but because England's great heroes of the naval fight against Spain – Drake, Raleigh, Howard and others – came from Devon. The building of the Royal Naval Dockyard at Devonport a century later ensured the prosperity of the great city in its beautiful harbour setting. History, as much as the sea-bathing, brought the Victorians to Plymouth, eager to walk in the steps of Drake on Plymouth Hoe and to explore Charles II's great Citadel.*

BELOW, RIGHT: *The training ship Impregnable, a three-decker of Nelson's day, moored in Plymouth Harbour. At the end of the 19th century, Plymouth, with the naval dockyard at Devonport, was the principal nursery of the British fleet – still the greatest in the world, despite the naval ambitions of Queen Victoria's German nephew, Kaiser Wilhelm II.*

RIGHT: *Although it would not be completed until 1910, the great cathedral at the heart of Truro still dominates this view of Cornwall's administrative centre. The cathedral, surrounded by Georgian buildings in the town centre, was built around the 16th-century parish church, with work beginning in 1880. It was the first Protestant cathedral to be built in England since St Paul's, in London, was completed in the 17th century.*

LEFT: *St Michael's Mount, in Mount Bay, off Penzance in Cornwall. The privately-owned island, once a place of pilgrimage and which legend says is all that remains of King Arthur's lost city of Lyonesse, was visited by Queen Victoria and Prince Albert in 1846. This major event in the Mount's history was commemorated by a metal tablet set up near the east pier, and by a brass footprint marking the spot where the Queen set her foot on landing.*

LEFT: *A fine view of the harbour and town of Falmouth. When Henry VIII built Pendennis Castle at Falmouth in 1538, he ensured that the excellent harbour in west Cornwall would have a good future as a shipping town. In the late 19th century, others got their eye on Falmouth, with builders quickly developing the "many eligible building sites and erecting thereon large and commodious houses and charming terraces". Falmouth was now a resort.*

ABOVE: *The Logan Rock, the most famous piece of rock in Cornwall. On a headland of the high granite cliffs on Cornwall's south coast near Land's End, the Logan Rock is a huge boulder weighing something like 66 tons, that can be made to wobble with nothing more serious than a hefty push. After a young naval lieutenant and a party of sailors pushed it over in 1824, and were ordered by the Admiralty to put it back at their expense, no one tried the trick again.*

LEFT: *The Victorians came in their thousands to gaze upon England's most westerly point at Land's End. Here, high granite cliffs, ending in a spiny promontory, reached into the wild Atlantic Ocean "like the snout of an alligator", as a guidebook of the period put it. More than a mile out to sea, the granite-built Longships Lighthouse could be seen on its cluster of rocks, its lantern beaming a warning to shipping.*

LEFT: *La Corbière Lighthouse, built on La Corbière Rock in Jersey, in the Channel Islands, in 1874. At low water, Victorians could visit the lighthouse, reaching it by train from St Aubin, and having first obtained a permit from the secretariat at the Hotel de Ville. They walked along a paved way, submerged at high tide, and climbed 95 steps up the rock to the entrance to the lighthouse. It was quite an adventure, especially for ladies with long skirts.*

ABOVE: *Hugh Town (or Houghton), on St Mary's, the largest island of the Scilly Isles. The Scilly Isles, out in the Atlantic nearly 35 miles (56 km) from Land's End, were difficult for Victorians to get to. As an 1890s guidebook said, "In visiting these islands care should be taken to employ only experienced boatmen, and to secure good boats. The rocks, winds and currents are sufficiently dangerous to require strangers to be extremely cautious."*

ABOVE: *On the quay at Padstow, on the Camel estuary on the north Cornish coast. By the 1890s, Padstow's best days as a fishing port and harbour handling many different cargoes, including some from across the Atlantic, were in the past. The shifting sands of the estuary made navigation difficult for the larger ships of the late 19th century. A railway line reached Padstow in 1899, too late to revive trade but at least able to take fish quickly to bigger markets.*

OPPOSITE: *Boscastle, on Cornwall's north coast. Despite its deep, narrow harbour, Boscastle was a busy little port in the 19th century, shipping out locally quarried slate. The village had few historical associations, apart from a grassy mound on which a castle had once stood. As no one was yet ready to play up legends of King Arthur and Tingtagel, four miles away along a hilly road, or of Cornish witchcraft, Boscastle remained a quiet, un-touristy place.*

RIGHT: *A ship in the only lock on the 35-mile (54-km)-long Bude–Launceston Canal. Before it had a share in the late 19th-century promotion of the north Cornish coast as one long health resort, Bude's main claim to fame was this canal. Opened in 1823, it was used to carry sea sand inland for farm fertilization and brought back to Bude harbour oats and slate. Soon after this picture was taken, the canal fell into disuse, made redundant by the railway.*

LEFT: *The tide is out in the harbour at Clovelly, west along the north Devon coast from Bideford. Fishing boats are drawn up on the shoreline, within the sheltering wall of the 18th-century stone quay. When the harbour was filled with the local, red-sailed fishing boats, it presented a very attractive sight, much appreciated by the village's many visitors.*

BELOW: *Ilfracombe, in north Devon, was a busy little harbour and fishing port until the railway started bringing flocks of tourists to its attractive setting and its small, rock-strewn beaches nestling beneath steep cliffs. By the 1890s, the guide books were calling Ilfracombe the chief and most beautiful watering-place on the north Devon coast and the 18th-century jetty was being called a pier.*

OPPOSITE: *The High Street of delightful little Clovelly, built up a cliff on the north Devon coast, was so steep that donkeys were employed to carry people down to the harbour – and back up again. That visitors could enjoy the delights of the village in the late 19th century was due to Christine Hamlyn, who owned the Clovelly Estate and devoted herself from the 1880s until her death in 1936 to restoring and preserving its many fine old buildings.*

CHAPTER FIVE

MIDLANDS

For English people in the age of Queen Victoria, the Midlands – the middle counties, between the south and the increasingly industrialized north – were the heart of the country, emotionally as well as geographically. Stretching from counties bordering Wales in the west to Lincolnshire and the east coast between the Wash and the Humber, the Midlands was a region of fine old market towns, to which generations of farmers had brought their goods, and of magnificent cathedrals, from Gloucester in the west to Lincoln in the east, where Christians had worshipped for centuries. And there were miraculously preserved medieval towns like Chester contrasting with much more recently established watering-places, from elegant Cheltenham in Gloucestershire to bracing and rather brash Skegness in Lincolnshire.

ABOVE: *The Rows, a series of 14th-century galleried streets in Chester. The best-preserved walled city in England, Chester in the 19th century was long past its maritime heyday, the River Dee having silted up, and the shipping trade had moved to Liverpool.*

RIGHT: *Westgate Street, one of the main streets of Gloucester. Built by the Romans as a fortification of the route to Wales, Gloucester in the 19th century was a busy market and manufacturing town, proud of its glorious cathedral.*

LEFT: *The Pittville Gardens in Cheltenham. The small, medieval Cotswolds town blossomed around an alkaline spring, discovered in a field in the 18th century. Soon, Cheltenham, helped by a visit from George III, was one of England's finest spa towns. Much of the town's architecture was Regency, including the splendidly domed and colonnaded Pittville Pump Room, set in an elegantly laid-out park, with wide lawns and lakes shaded by splendid trees.*

OPPOSITE: *The broad, tree-lined Promenade, looking towards the High Street, in Cheltenham. Laid out early in the 19th century, the Promenade was lined with a fine terrace incorporating Ionic columns. It was perhaps all this Classicism that made the Victorians think that Cheltenham was a good place to found schools. Two public schools, Cheltenham College and Cheltenham Ladies College, were established in the town in the 19th century.*

ABOVE: *The splendid Market Cross in Lydney, Gloucestershire. In medieval markets, the market cross was the place where traders paid their tolls and taxes and where the official weights and measures were often kept. It was not until the 19th century that Britain got an official, nationwide system of weights and measures. The 1878 Weights and Measures Act decreed that a yard (0.91 metre) was the measure marked on a metal bar kept at the Guildhall in London.*

BELOW: *The splendid local red sandstone Market House in Ross-on-Wye in Herefordshire.
Ross was granted its first market charter by King Stephen in 1138. Later, the Thursday charter
market was extended by a statute market on Saturdays, both days still being busy market days
in Victorian Ross. The massively pillared Market House was built for the town by the Dowager
Duchess of Somerset in 1670; the neat clock tower came later.*

LEFT: *Harvest time in the Malvern Hills, west of the River Severn in Worcestershire. Six towns and villages with "Malvern" in their name cluster in these hills. The biggest of them, Great Malvern, became a spa town in Victorian times when enterprising local people began bottling the pure spring water found in the Malvern Hills. Soon, Malvern Water was finding its way into the best houses in Britain and was being shipped throughout the Empire.*

ABOVE: *A pleasure boat comes through the arches of the Severn Bridge at Worcester. The city's magnificent cathedral rises beyond the bridge. Most Victorians knew Worcester best for two widely different things. First was an exceptionally beautiful porcelain, the first porcelain factory having been set up in the city in the mid-18th century. The second was a condiment, Worcestershire Sauce, which two local men, Messrs Lea and Perrins, began making in 1825.*

ABOVE: *Clive of India gazes across The Square in Shrewsbury. After achieving fame and fortune in India – and later losing both – Robert Clive, who was born near Shrewsbury, was the town's MP for many years, and mayor in 1762. Charles Darwin, also born and educated in Shrewsbury, was perhaps a more controversial figure in his home town in the 19th century. His theories on evolution and the origin of species caused great argument when his famous book was published in 1859.*

RIGHT: *A horse-drawn tram makes its way along Eastgate Street in Chester. Many of Chester's ancient streets had "gate" in their names, an indication of the importance of the city's great walls in its early history. The city's red sandstone walls, complete with gate towers and ramparts, were built, partly on the Romans' original fortifications, in the 10th century, after centuries of raids by Danes and Saxons had almost reduced the town to ruins.*

ABOVE: *The impressive Tudor Gothic gateway called the Stonebow and the Guildhall (above the gate) in the High Street in Lincoln. The great cathedral city, built on a limestone ridge at the junction of two major Roman roads, Ermine Street and the Fosse Way, had, by the 19th century, become a quiet city in the midst of flat farmland.*

OPPOSITE: *The pleasure pier at Skegness, marching out to sea across the firm white sands of the Lincolnshire seaside resort. Excursionists, tiring of the entertainments on the sands, which, during the season, included donkeys, swings, "cocoanut" shies, and beach photographers, could buy a ticket for the pier. Once at the end of the pier, they could enjoy entertainments or simply have a cup of tea in the large pavilion.*

RIGHT: *The Parade and Clock Tower at Skegness, the most important watering place on the Lincolnshire coast. Older folk, coming to Skegness in the late 1870s after an absence of some years, would not have recognized it, for it was developed rapidly after the railway arrived in 1873. Broad, villa-lined streets, public gardens, parades, hotels with assembly rooms capable of holding 1000 people and a long pier were all built in less than a decade.*

CHAPTER SIX

EAST ANGLIA

This chapter, using the term "East Anglia" in a broad sense, looks at England's eastern counties, including, as well as Norfolk and Suffolk, Cambridgeshire and Bedfordshire. A land of reed-edged lakes and waterways, drained by many rivers and streams, in the 19th century this was a quiet country, the great vistas of farmland in Bedfordshire rolling over low hills and into the flatlands of the Bedford Levels, the Cambridgeshire Fens and the Norfolk Broads. At the coastal edge, jutting out into a cold sea where the breezes were "bracing", there was more noise and activity, as the Victorians rapidly turned old fishing ports into exciting new resorts.

LEFT: *Boats moored at Sportman's Staithe (or "landing stage") on Ormesby Broad. The Norfolk Broads, for centuries tucked away below sea level behind the East Anglian coast, became popular sailing and boating places for Victorians.*

ABOVE: *Gonville and Caius College and the Senate House, Cambridge. Founded in the 13th century, the university transformed itself in the 19th century from a slackly disciplined place for the sons of gentlemen to one of the world's great centres of learning.*

BELOW: *Great Yarmouth in the late 19th century was the most important town and port on the East Anglian coast. For most of the year, it carried on its life as a busy port and fishing industry town, with a large, centuries-old market. During the summer holiday season, Great Yarmouth was transformed into what a guide book of the period called a "saturnalia…filled with what one may term the concentrated essence of Bank Holiday".*

LEFT: *The firm, extensive sands at Great Yarmouth. A marine parade, three piers, a revolving tower offering views over land and sea, an aquarium and, off the sands, a Theatre Royal, all vied for the attention of holidaymakers. There were plenty of sailing craft to give them a spin out to sea, and a large regatta offered a spectacular climax to the August holiday season.*

BELOW: *The South Pier at Great Yarmouth. In the 1890s, Great Yarmouth boasted three piers. The oldest was the Wellington Pier, which was opened in 1853 and named after the Duke of Wellington, who had died the year before. The town's monument to Norfolk's favourite son, Horatio Nelson, another hero of the Napoleonic Wars, was erected in 1819.*

ABOVE: *The pier head and jetty at Lowestoft, considered by Victorians to be the chief watering-place of Suffolk. Centuries of rivalry between the town and Great Yarmouth – they were on opposite sides in the Civil War and had fought for domination over the herring industry for years. Lowestoft felt they had won because their resort was much more select than their brash and noisy rival up the coast in Norfolk.*

LEFT: *The Terrace, a recently built row of housing in "the usual style of watering-place architecture" at Lowestoft. It is an indication of how the old East Anglian town and fishing port pulled itself into the 19th century in order to attract the very profitable holiday crowds brought to them by the railways. The railway companies also had an interest in improving trade: Lowestoft's new fish market at the head of the north pier was built by the Great Eastern Railway Company in 1865.*

Yachtsmen had to lower their masts – and their heads – to get under the single-lane humped-back bridge at Potter Heigham, near Hickling Broad. The village shops catered for all the needs of people wanting to mess about in boats on the Broads.

ABOVE: *A tranquil scene on the river at Barton Broad. One of the five major Broads of the Norfolk Broads, Barton Broad was on the Ant river, in the north-west of the area. Coarse fishing was the order of the day on the Broads.*

BELOW: *Readying a sailing boat near the bridge at Wroxham, near Wroxham Broad. At the western edge of the Norfolk Broads, Wroxham provided an array of shops and services for visitors, and also hired out various kinds of craft and offered boat trips on the linked rivers, lakes and streams, as well as man-made waterways, that made up the Broads.*

OPPOSITE: *The Bridge of Sighs over the River Cam at St John's College in Cambridge. An enclosed stone bridge built in 1831, it was originally called New Bridge. Its resemblance to the famous bridge between the Doge's Palace and the prisons in Venice ensured that it was very quickly re-named.*

ABOVE: *King's College, Cambridge, named after Henry VI, who founded it in 1441. The reason why so many empty carriages are drawn up outside is probably because their occupants have gone into King's to visit its glorious chapel (in the centre of the picture). One of the finest examples of Perpendicular Gothic architecture in England, the chapel also had brilliantly coloured stained-glass and superb fan tracery in its stone roof.*

RIGHT: *Girton College, Cambridge. Like its rival, Oxford, Cambridge University, albeit reluctantly, admitted women during the 19th century. Girton College, originally an establishment in Hitchen to prepare women for the Cambridge Previous Examination and Ordinary Degree, was moved to Girton, two miles outside Cambridge, in 1874. It was another six years before women were allowed to sit the same Tripos examinations as men.*

LEFT: *The Promenade, Bedford. The county town of Bedfordshire, Bedford developed along both banks of the Great Ouse river, one of the important navigation rivers of England's eastern counties. In the centre of the town, numerous pleasant tree-lined walks stretched along the river banks. From The Promenade, boats could be hired for a quiet hour or two on the river.*

ABOVE: *A statue to John Howard, the 18th-century prison reformer, in Bedford. Captured by a French privateer on his way to Lisbon, Howard spent enough time in prison to get a good idea of how inhuman imprisonment could be. Back in England, he settled at Cardington, near Bedford, becoming high sheriff for Bedfordshire in 1773. He made a series of tours of British prisons, and his reports led to two acts of parliament improving prison conditions.*

CHAPTER SEVEN

NORTHERN ENGLAND

The Victorians knew the north of England as a region of many contrasting glories. Ancient market towns and cathedral cities shared a country of moors, heaths and dales, rolling pastureland and rugged hills with the great smoke-belching cities and ports of the Industrial Revolution. From Blackpool and the Isle of Man on the Atlantic Ocean to Scarborough and Whitby on the German Ocean, from the wildly beautiful Derbyshire Peak District to the loveliness of the Lake District, the Victorians explored it all, more often than not on the railways which, as the 19th century progressed, spread a network of lines to all parts of the region.

ABOVE: *Donkeys on the sands at Blackpool. Donkeys made an early appearance at the seaside, being at Brighton in the late 18th century. Gipsies are thought to have first had the idea of hirng out donkeys on the sands and promenades.*

RIGHT: *Blackpool's sands, seen from the North Pier. The Tower, Blackpool's version of Paris' Eiffel Tower, was the tallest building in Britain when it opened in 1894, and the big wheel was a copy of one at Coney Island, in America.*

ABOVE: *Stepping stones across the Dove in Dovedale, Derbyshire. In the 19th century the Derbyshire Peak District was a popular destination for travellers seeking the romance of wild places: Jane Austen sent Elizabeth Bennet there, for instance. Dovedale suited the most exacting requirements, having its fair share of Lover's Leaps, mysterious caves and spectacular rock formations, all on a stretch of the River Dove that flowed through a limestone gorge.*

RIGHT: *The stylish entrance, complete with roof garden, to the Pump Room in the Derbyshire spa town of Buxton. The 5th Duke of Devonshire had the idea of rivalling Bath in his own territory and at the end of the 18th century put up a stylish Crescent in Buxton, opposite a hot spring. By the mid-19th century, Buxton was flourishing, helped by the fact that its spring waters, charged with nitrogen and carbon gas, were actually quite pleasant to drink.*

LEFT: *The art gallery and museum in Liverpool. The Walker Art Gallery was the gift to the city of Sir Andrew Barclay Walker, Liverpool's Lord Mayor in 1873. When it opened, it housed the nucleus of what would become the largest collection of paintings in Britain outside London, including works by George Stubbs, who was born in the city.*

OPPOSITE: *St George's Hall in Liverpool. This Greco-Roman-style building was one of the Victorian Age's finest contributions to the architecture of Liverpool. It was designed by a young architect called Lonsdale Elmes, who was just 24 when the Hall's foundation stone was laid in 1838, the year after Victoria's accession. St George's Hall was completed in 1854.*

ABOVE: *New Brighton Beach, across the Mersey estuary from Liverpool. The chief seaside resort on the Mersey estuary, New Brighton lost as much as it gained by being so close to the great commercial city and port. It had everything a good resort should have, including a commodious pier and a sandy beach well supplied with all sorts of entertainments. But it was slightly grubby and rather scruffy and only came really alive on Bank Holidays.*

ABOVE: *The West End Pier at Morecambe. It is a windy day and quite a rough sea is blowing in from Morecambe Bay. Guide books of the period tended to look down on Morecambe, largely because it was visited mostly by day trippers from the busy industrial towns of Lancashire and Yorkshire – "for whose recreation are provided abundant entertainments of a distinctly popular order", as one guide book put it rather sniffily.*

RIGHT: *The Parade at Morecambe, looking west towards the promenade pier. The pier, opened in 1869, was built entirely of iron. The iron railings, lamp stands and decorations were probably not designed specifically for the pier. It is more likely that the local borough surveyor chose them from the catalogue of one of the great Victorian foundaries, many of which produced very large and varied ranges of cast-iron designs.*

RIGHT: *The bridge and pier at Southport. This stylish resort, just half an hour's ride by train from Liverpool, had managed to make itself a little more exclusive and rather less noisy than Blackpool, its near-neighbour up the coast. Its pier was exceptionally long – which it needed to be as the sea had been retreating from Southport for years – it had built two artificial lakes for safe boating and offered land-yachting on its broad, firm sands in summer.*

RIGHT: *Blackpool's North Pier, said to be "the more select" of the resort's two large piers. Whereas the South Pier was just a "penny pier" where dancing went on all day in the summer, the North Pier made itself more selective by charging more than a penny for entry, although it also offered a good selection of entertainments and amusement stalls and two pavilions at its head.*

BELOW: *On the crowded sands at Blackpool, with the North Pier in the background. At low-tide, when the sea had retreated a long way out, Blackpool's sands stretched for nearly 20 miles along the coast, offering an enormous playground for the working classes of Lancashire's industrial towns. They came in their thousands, often on day-trip outings organized by their employers, with very few of them able to afford special holiday clothes.*

OPPOSITE: *It must be a Bank Holiday, or perhaps a Lancashire Wakes Week holiday, so crowded are the sands at Blackpool. The 520-foot (839-metre)-high Blackpool Tower, soaring into the sky above the sands, remained Britain's tallest building for many years after it opened in 1894.*

RIGHT: *The charming little station for the electric tourist train at Laxey, on the Isle of Man. The unusual attraction that brought Victorian tourists to Laxey was the giant Lady Isabella water wheel, the biggest of its kind in the world. The wheel, named after the wife of the island's Lieutenant Governor, began working in 1854 to keep nearby lead mines free of water.*

OPPOSITE: *The promenade at Douglas, capital of the Isle of Man. From the beginning of the 19th century, Douglas set out to make itself a desirable holiday place, and succeeded admirably. The first of its three piers was built in 1801 and two more had followed by mid-century. The Loch Parade, along the seafront, opened in 1877 and included a tramway along it.*

ABOVE: *The beach at Douglas, Isle of Man, at low-tide. Douglas prided itself on the excellence of its hotels, many of which were built along the promenade that edged the beach. Castle Mona, the very large, turreted building, backed by trees, a little away from the main line of buildings, was built by John, Duke of Atholl, the last of the Lords of Man. By the 1890s, the castle had become a hotel.*

ABOVE: *An idyllic pastoral scene in the Lake District: cattle in Derwent Water, the largest of the lakes in the western Lake District. This area was particularly popular with the Victorians because the wildest and most rugged of the Lake District's peaks and crags were to be found here. Greta Hall in Keswick, between Derwent Water and Bassenthwaite Lake, had been the home of the poet laureate Robert Southey for many years.*

OPPOSITE: *Windermere, viewed from the Ferry Hotel at Bowness, a popular Lake District tourist centre. The small steam ferry at the lake's edge took people to places all round the lake and to those of the lake's 14 islands that were open to the public.*

RIGHT: *A steam-driven ferry takes a large four-horse coach across Windermere. Many steam-driven ferry services operated in the Lake District, cutting down considerably on the time it would have taken to get by road from one side of the larger lakes to the other.*

RIGHT: *The Citadel, Carlisle. This imposing building, the last of the fortifications that centuries of existence on the border with Scotland had made necessary at Carlisle, was built by Henry VIII. By the late 19th century, when Carlisle had long ceased to be a garrison town and had become instead a prosperous textile-producing centre, the Citadel housed an assize court and county offices.*

BELOW: *The Market Place, Carlisle. As well as having a charter market, Carlisle was able to proclaim a Great Fair for the first time in 1352. This fair was always proclaimed from the market cross in the market place. Carlisle Cross was rebuilt in 1682 and it is this Cross, a column set on stone steps, that can be seen at the top of this picture, to the left of the statue in front of the 18th-century Old Town Hall.*

LEFT: *The Old Mill at Jesmond Dene, Newcastle-upon-Tyne. The city built many fine parks and gardens for its citizens during the 19th century. Jesmond Dene, to the north-east of the city, was one of the most attractive of them.*

OPPOSITE: *On the beach at Tynemouth, near Newcastle upon Tyne. Connected to the smoky industrial city by a branch of the North-Eastern Railway, Tynemouth offered Newcastle a breath of fresh air on a beach where many rockpools provided lots of fun for children. Other attractions were the Aquarium and Winter Gardens, in a large building by the sands, a switchback railway and a fine public park.*

ABOVE: *A railway line embankment and bridge, sign of Newcastle's industrial might, passes between two relics of the city's massive Norman castle, the Keep and the 13th-century Black Gate. During the Victorian Age the old centre of Newcastle was rebuilt and transformed into one of the finest city centres in Britain. Queen Victoria herself came up to Newcastle in 1850 to open the monumental Central Railway Station.*

RIGHT: *The gaunt ruins of 13th-century Whitby Abbey dominate the East Cliff at Whitby, Yorkshire. A prosperous port in the 18th century, with a whaling fleet, a base for colliers and a ship-building yard that turned out both of Captain James Cook's ships, Whitby by the late 19th century was very much a fishing port and seaside resort. Jewellery carved from jet found along the cliffs near Whitby was very popular with Victorian visitors.*

ABOVE: *A maze of steep lanes and alleyways separating small cottages, the ancient fishing village of Staithes, on the north Yorkshire coast, tumbles dizzily down a cliff to the tiny harbour. Victorians came here on excursions from Whitby because it was an attractive fishing village, with spectacular views of the cliffs, and because the "celebrated circumnavigator of the globe", Captain Cook, was apprenticed to a grocer here.*

BELOW: *Robin Hood's Bay, Yorkshire, the destination of many excursions from Whitby. The bay and attractive little fishing village got their name from a legend that arrows shot by Robin Hood and Little John from the tower of Whitby Abbey landed on two spots in nearby Hawsker, later marked by two upright stones. The famous outlaw was supposed to have fled to Robin Hood's Bay from Sherwood Forest to avoid capture.*

BELOW: *The Spa at Scarborough in Yorkshire. Scarborough was the first town in England where "taking the waters", by drinking water from a mineral spring and – more important – by sea-bathing, was practised for health reasons. The first bathing machines also appeared on the sands at Scarborough, in the 1730s. By the mid-19th century, Scarborough, by now a very stylish and fashionable place, was advertising itself as "the Queen of English Watering Places".*

LEFT: *The Children's Corner, on the sands at Scarborough. Many resorts, if their sands were extensive enough, set aside special areas for children, with their mothers or nannies. At Scarborough, the Children's Corner was set in an area, with some interesting seaweed-strewn rocks and pools, south of the Spa and conveniently close to the South Cliffs Tramway.*

ABOVE: *The Children's Corner at Bridlington. Considered a less pretentious resort than Scarborough, a few miles away round Flamborough Head, Bridlington was also a good deal less expensive and so was popular with families. Backing the fine, firm sands was a promenade with gardens, a band stand and various pavilions and tea places – ideal for a quiet holiday.*

ABOVE: *Skipton Castle, Yorkshire. This great castle, built by the powerful Yorkshire family, the Cliffords, so far from being outside the market town of Skipton, was right at the top of the busy High Street. Parts of the castle were Norman, but it had been extensively rebuilt later, parts of it as recently as the 17th century. Thus, in the 19th century, it was more of a comfortable house than a serious fortification.*

OPPOSITE: *Scarborough Castle, Yorkshire. This had once been a very large Norman castle, dominating the headland that the town developed on and around. By the time Scarborough had earned its reputation as a queen of watering-places, the castle had long been a ruin. Visitors, climbing Castle Hill to take in the extensive views over the German Ocean, could see the remains of an ancient chapel in the castle yard, and a water reservoir, the Lady's Well.*

ABOVE: *The Prospect Hotel at Harrogate, in north Yorkshire. At the beginning of the 19th century, Harrogate was the most fashionably exclusive spa town in the north of England. Although the growth of such seaside spas as Scarborough somewhat diminished Harrogate's popularity, it still drew large enough numbers of visitors to its Royal Pump Room, Royal Baths and well laid-out gardens to make it essential for large hotels, such as the one in the centre of this picture, to be built in the town.*

LEFT: *Sunday afternoon in the Valley Gardens, Harrogate. These gardens, established in a natural valley that sheltered them from winds, were in the fashionable heart of Harrogate, near the Royal Pump Room and Baths. In summer, there were concerts from the band stand, and for much of the year, visitors could enjoy a stroll along the Sun Colonnade, a glass-covered walkway.*

ABOVE: *York and its magnificent Minster seen from the city walls. York Minster, the largest Gothic church in England, was built between the 13th and 15th centuries. The 19th century's contribution to the Minster's history involved two disastrous fires in 1829 and 1839. After the first, which did great damage in the choir, new stalls were designed by the architect, Sir Robert Smirke, designer of the British Museum in London.*

OPPOSITE: *Micklegate Bar, one of the four medieval gates into the city of York, still intact centuries after it was built. Much of York's ramparts remained for Victorians to walk along as they contemplated the great changes that came when York, led by its charismatic Lord Mayor, George Husdon, cashed in on the railway boom in Britain and became very rich. York Station, just outside the city walls, was very grand indeed, and quite cathedral-like with its iron pillars, vaulted in iron and glass.*

CHAPTER EIGHT

SOUTH WALES

The Industrial Revolution really got into its stride in south Wales in the 19th century. The valleys of the south-east, with their extensive coal deposits, became the source of the power that drove iron foundaries, ship-building yards and docks (and the ships they built), factories and mills in Wales and England. Away from the valleys, the pace of life was quieter, though few places were left totally undisturbed by Victorian progress – the ever-growing railway system made sure of that. Some grew considerably, especially if they were well situated to take advantage of the Victorian fondness for seaside holidays and exploring historic sites.

ABOVE: *Kidwelly Castle, on Carmarthen Bay, was immense when it was completed in the 14th century. Even in its ruined state 400 years later, there still remained a semi-circular moat and an inner courtyard with a circular tower at each corner.*

RIGHT: *On the seafront at Aberystwyth, the home of the University College of Wales. On the west coast of Wales, the town saw a rapid improvement in its amenities, from a new marine terrace to a pure water supply, after the railway arrived in mid-century.*

RIGHT: *Cardiff's rebuilt old castle looked down on a city whose industrial regeneration was fuelled by coal from the valleys of south Wales. When the Bute West Dock was opened at Cardiff in 1839, to be linked shortly after by rail to pits and ironworks inland, the town began a rapid period of growth. Within decades, it was the greatest seaport in Wales.*

BELOW: *Cardiff Castle, seen here from the east, dated back to the first decades after the Norman Conquest. By the 1890s, the period of the picture, the castle owed much of its size and shape to two Marquises of Bute. The 2nd Marquis of Bute began pulling the old town into the Industrial Age in 1839 when he began building new docks on the quayside. His son, enriched like Cardiff itself, turned his attention to the ruins of the old castle in the 1870s.*

LEFT: *Women dressed in national costume display the wool they have spun, using the spinning wheel they stand beside. Wool from Welsh sheep provided the material for an important local industry in the 19th century. Traditionally-patterned, woven, wool blankets and other items became very desirable objects in Victorian homes.*

ABOVE: *The market town of Abergavenny, spread out along a mountain-encircled valley of the River Usk in Monmouthshire. Rising behind the town is Holy Mountain, one of a whole group of mountains rising to nearly 2000 feet (3225 metres). In Victorian times, Abergavenny was quietly prosperous, separated by the Brecon Beacons from the great industrial valleys of south Wales.*

BELOW: *The ruins of the castle at Abergavenny, tidied up and with railings to prevent visitors falling from them, and set amidst well-kept gardens. It must have taken quite a leap of the imagination to accept that this quiet place was the scene of one of the most savage massacres in Welsh history. In 1175, a Norman lord, William de Braose, revenged the murder of his uncle by inviting local chieftains to have Christmas Dinner with him in the castle. Once they were seated round the table, he slaughtered them all. On the orders of Charles I, the castle was reduced to ruins in 1645 to prevent it falling into Cromwell's hands.*

LEFT: *Still surrounded by the remains of its great moat, ruined Caerphilly Castle stands in the centre of Caerphilly. The town was better known to Victorians for its fine, crumbly cheese sold in the town's market than for the castle, the largest of the many massive fortifications built in Wales during the conquest of the country by the Normans.*

BELOW: *Raglan Castle, near Monmouth, achieved its greatest glory in its last days as a habitable castle. During the English Civil War, the Royalist 5th Earl of Worcester, whose family home the castle had been for several generations, held out in there for ten weeks against the troops of Oliver Cromwell. Raglan was the last castle to fall to Cromwell.*

ABOVE: *To romantically sensitive Victorians, Tintern Abbey was a very special place. Set in quietly beautiful country on a bend of the River Wye, the ruined abbey was more than just one of the finest remains of Britain's monastic past. It was a place for contemplation and for musing on the nature of humanity, as the young William Wordsworth had done in his "Lines composed a few miles above Tintern Abbey".*

RIGHT: *The church at Wonastow, a small village south of Monmouth. Like many churches in the area, Wonastow's church could be dated back to Saxon times.*

LEFT: *Kidwelly, south of Carmarthen, with the splendid ruins of its immense castle rising above the River Gwendraeth. Built in the 13th and 14th centuries, Kidwelly Castle was placed at a narrow, and therefore, defensible, point just before the river widened out into an estuary that flowed into Carmarthen Bay .*

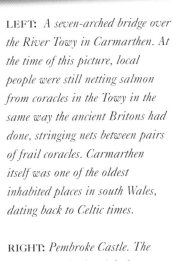

LEFT: *A seven-arched bridge over the River Towy in Carmarthen. At the time of this picture, local people were still netting salmon from coracles in the Towy in the same way the ancient Britons had done, stringing nets between pairs of frail coracles. Carmarthen itself was one of the oldest inhabited places in south Wales, dating back to Celtic times.*

RIGHT: *Pembroke Castle. The town of Pembroke might be small, but its Norman castle, set on a headland surrounded by water on three sides, was massive. Early in the 19th century, the Royal Naval Dockyard at Milford Haven was moved up the estuary to Pembroke Dock, and Pembroke benefited greatly as the dock built warships, and three royal yachts for Queen Victoria.*

ABOVE: *Tenby, an attractive little fishing harbour and resort in southwest Wales. As early as 1724, Daniel Defoe had described Tenby "as the most agreeable town on all the south coast of Wales, except Pembroke", and the Victorians agreed with him. As a seaside resort, its season lasted from June to October, and many people stayed there in the winter, so mild was its climate.*

LEFT: *Bathing machines line up at the water's edge on Tenby's South Sands. Tenby had two beaches, North and South Sands, both of which were well supplied with all the amenities expected of a seaside resort considered to be the most fashionable and well-favoured in Wales. The beaches were separated by the fishing and pleasure-boat harbour and by Castle Hill.*

BELOW: *The harbour at Tenby, seen from a path round Castle Hill, which had been turned into a visitor attraction. It had pleasant walks offering magnificent views and a terrace surmounted by a larger-than-lifesize statue of Prince Albert, the Prince Consort. The remaining un-ruined part of the Norman castle, its keep, was used in the 19th century as a signal station by the Preventive (that is, anti-smuggling) Service.*

LEFT: *Aberystwyth, from Constitution Hill. Set half way down the coast of Cardigan Bay, Aberystwyth's development into a busy, thriving town during the 19th century, was greatly helped by the coming of the railway. Two major Welsh cultural institutions were opened there in the 1870s. The University College of Wales was established in a turretted, gothic-style building on the seafront in 1872, and the National Library of Wales followed a year later.*

BELOW: *On the Terrace at Aberystwyth. Not the most popular of Welsh seaside resorts, despite choosing to advertise itself as "the Queen of Welsh Watering Places", Aberystwyth still offered a pleasant, if quiet, time to its visitors. Apart from a pier and a promenade, its greatest attraction was its ruined castle, set amidst gardens on a rocky promontory on the seafront. A favourite excursion was to the Devil's Fall and Bridge, 12 miles (20 km) away.*

CHAPTER NINE

NORTH WALES

Great contrasts abounded in 19th-century north Wales, a land of mighty castles, deep slate quarries, rivers flowing down beautiful, wooded valleys, and fine old towns, many of them dominated by the sky-reaching presence of Snowdon, the highest mountain in England and Wales. Perhaps the greatest contrasts were those made by the century's railway boom. The swift spread of the railway in Wales rapidly turned small fishing villages on the north coast into large, vibrant seaside resorts, made possible a great increase the production and export of slate, and, by the end of the century, was even taking people in comfort to the top of Snowdon.

ABOVE: *A fisherman with his coracle on the River Dee at Llangollen. The town, at the head of the lovely Vale of Llangollen, was famous in the 19th century as the home of the clever, independently-minded and hospitable "Ladies of Llangollen".*

RIGHT: *Llandudno, stretched out along Llandudno Bay, was the largest seaside resort in Wales. The town's well-named Happy Valley was where many of the entertainments, including minstrel shows, entertainers and bands, were to be found.*

LEFT: *Harlech Castle, one of the great ring of castles built by Edward I to contain the Welsh. Built by the sea on Tremadog Bay and protected by a wide moat on the side away from the sea, Harlech Castle played stirring roles in many of the dramas of Welsh history. Henry V captured Owen Glendower's wife and children here, and the castle was besieged in both the Wars of the Roses and the Civil War.*

ABOVE: *Barmouth, on the Mawddach Estuary. Rather than a pier, this south-west facing, sea-bathing town had a railway bridge, nearly a mile long, along which ran a fine promenade offering breathtaking views of sea and hills, especially at high-tide or sunset. Bathing on Barmouth sands was well organized, with separate bathing places set aside for women and for men.*

BELOW: *The halt at Tan-y-Bwlch, on the Ffestiniog Railway. The narrow-gauge railway was built in the mid-19th century to carry slate from the quarries at Blaenau Ffestiniog down to Porthmadog. By the 1890s, about 100,000 tons of slate from the Ffestiniog quarries was being exported from Porthmadog every year. The railway did not carry tourist traffic and attractions like Snowdon and Beddgelert were reached by coach from Porthmadog.*

RIGHT: *The Fairy Glen at Betwys-y-Coed. The English landscape painter, David Cox, alerted Victorians to the many beauties of Snowdonia. Cox was in his early 20s when he visited north Wales, and the area remained a life-long favourite sketching place. And no wonder, with such beauties as the Swallow Falls, Fairy Glen and Conwy Falls all within walking distance of Betwys-y-Coed, a resort developed to serve visitors to the loveliest part of Snowdonia.*

LEFT: *The start of the Lyn Perid Pass at Llanberis. This road led into the main Llanberis Pass, one of the scenically spectacular ways up to Snowdon. For most of the 19th century the way was tackled by horse-drawn coaches. Younger and more adventurous people could either walk or ride ponies up to the summit of the highest mountain in England and Wales.*

LEFT: *Caernarfon Castle. Edward I built his mighty castle on the Menai Strait on a very ancient site. His son, who became Edward II, was born in the castle and the king proclaimed him Prince of Wales there in 1284. The title has been held by the eldest son of the monarch ever since. Caernarfon's history and its position close to some of the finest scenery in north Wales ensured its popularity with visitors – who had to pay only a few pence to visit the great castle.*

BELOW: *The last mile of the railway at Snowdon. The rack-and-pinion steam railway that ran up Mount Snowdon from Llanberis was opened in 1896. The two-mile (8-km) train took tourists up to the summit of Mount Snowdon, often up gradients of 1 in 5. Since the easiest walk up to the summit also started from Llanberis, many Victorians chose to walk to the top.*

LEFT: *Slate quarries at Bethesda. This little town was built in the mid-18th century to house workers at the world's largest slate quarry, and took its name from the Nonconformist chapel there. A century later, it had found a second source of income, as a tourist resort in the centre of one of the most scenically spectacular parts of Snowdonia. The town was the starting point of the ascent of the Nant Ffrancon Pass, famed for its difficulty and for the splendour of its views.*

RIGHT: *Eight-towered Conwy Castle, the greatest of Edward I's castles in Wales. Built where the Conwy river reached the sea, the castle was a formidable defence against the rebellious Welsh princes. The medieval-looking suspension bridge was built more than five centuries after the castle. It was the work of the great Scottish engineer, Thomas Telford, who carefully designed the battlements of the bridge's supporting towers to match the turrets of the castle.*

ABOVE: *The beach front at Llandudno. Until the mid-19th century, Llandudno, on the north Wales coast, was a mining and fishing village. Then, two enterprising local men transformed it into a well-planned resort, with a wide promenade, a fine pier and lovely gardens. In 1862, it delighted the Liddell family, on holiday with their friend Charles Lutwidge Dodgson and their daughter, Alice, to whom Dodgson told stories.* Alice in Wonderland *grew out of the stories.*

BELOW: *The pier and pavilion at Colwyn Bay. On the rapidly developing coast of north Wales, Colwyn Bay was a thriving new town, not to be confused with the village of Colwyn, a short distance inland. Here, local people suddenly found their village being called "Old Colwyn", so it would not be confused with the smart new watering-place on the coast. Colwyn Bay was another resort made successful by a railway line, this time the Chester–Holyhead line.*

ABOVE: *The promenade pier at Rhyl, stalking out to sea across a shore that two or three decades before had known nothing more serious than a few fishermen's huts. Another rapidly growing north Wales coastal resort, Rhyl's closeness to Liverpool and Chester ensured it would have plenty of visitors as soon as the railway reached it. The pavilion at the entrance to the pier seated 2500 people, and had one of the largest organs in England (and Wales) behind the stage.*

BELOW: *Within the walls of the ruined Valle Crucis Abbey, to the north-west of Llangollen. A Cistercian foundation, the abbey was built at the beginning of the 13th century. The abbey ruins made a thought-provoking study in contrasts for people who might have just come from being shown over Plas Newydd, the large, attractively timbered home for 50 years (until 1831) of the eccentric "Ladies of Llangollen".*

LEFT: *The picturesque ruins of Rhuddlan Castle, at Rhuddlan, near Rhyl on the road to the small cathedral city of St Asaph. Rhyl was fortunate to have close to hand some very fine inland attractions to run excursions to. It was built at the mouth of the River Clwyd, which ran down to the sea through one of the prettiest valleys in north Wales. And Rhuddlan and St Asaph were both interesting towns.*

CHAPTER TEN

SOUTH-EAST SCOTLAND

Scotland's south-east corner, stretching from the supremely lovely, rolling hill and moor country of the Borders to the foot of the Highlands, is a region full of historical associations. The Victorians could visit places like Stirling and castles like Doune and still feel in the air a sense of the passions that had caused battles to be won and lost, and causes to be fought for. They could also note how their own age had brought a new look to many parts of this region, from Hawick in the Borders, where knitting had become an important export industry, to Portobello, where a retired naval officer's villa had given a name to a delightful new seaside resort.

ABOVE: *Bridge of Allen, on Allan Water, the river that inspired Robert Burns's lovely poem, "Banks of Allan Water". Bridge of Allan, near Stirling, was an attractive and elegant spa where Victorians went to take the saline waters.*

RIGHT: *Princes Street and the Princes Street Gardens in Edinburgh, with the Royal Scottish Academy ahead and Edinburgh Castle to the left. The picture was taken from the Scott Monument, which was built between 1840 and 1844.*

RIGHT: *The Scott Monument in Princes Street, Edinburgh. When this gloriously over-the-top monument was first mooted, shortly after his death in 1832, Sir Walter Scott was considered by many to be the greatest novelist ever and certainly Scotland's greatest literary figure. The monument, completed in 1844, was a wonderfully decorated and ornamented Gothic steeple, 180 feet (55 metres) high, with a large, but simply styled statue of Scott, seated with his deerhound Maida at his side, set beneath it.*

BELOW: *Holyrood Palace, with Arthur's Seat in the background. This palace of the kings of Scotland in Edinburgh was built on the site of an abbey called Holy Rood, founded in a forested valley below Arthur's Seat in the 12th century. Virtually ignored once the crowns of England and Scotland were united in 1603, Holyrood Palace came into its own again as a royal residence after the State Visit to Scotland of George IV in 1822, a visit that was largely engineered and orchestrated by Sir Walter Scott.*

ABOVE: *The promenade pier at Portobello. The small town, almost a suburb of Edinburgh, to which it was linked by a tramway, became a popular seaside resort in mid-Victorian times. The great Scottish music-hall entertainer, Sir Harry Lauder, was born in Portobello in 1870, and it is pleasant to thank that he got his first breaths of sea air and healthy ozone on Portobello's pier.*

LEFT: *On the beach at Portobello. The town owed its rather exotic name to a retired naval officer, who had fought in the action to capture Porto Bello at Panama in the West Indies in 1739. When he built a villa for his retirement on the shore a few miles outside Edinburgh, he called it Portobello. Grown into a small town in Victorian times, Portobello could offer holidaymakers a fine marine parade along the sandy shore, where the bathing was pleasant, a pier, and an excellent golf links, where players wore red coats.*

LEFT: *The Martyrs' Monument, Stirling. A typical piece of Victorian marble near-bathos, this monument under a glass dome is a representation of the Wigtown Martyrs. The martyrs were two women Covenanters who, in 1685, were tied to a stake in the estuary at Wigtown and left to drown in the rising tide. Another monument to them was erected in Wigtown in 1858.*

BELOW: *Stirling Castle, on its crag above the town of Stirling, with public gardens and a public cemetery, built on the site of an old tilting ground, spread out below. Stirling Castle, at a strategically important point on the Forth river, was also a favoured residence of the Stewart kings. Mary, Queen of Scots, was crowned in the castle's chapel and her son, James VI, was baptised there.*

LEFT: *The Wallace Monument in Stirling, a Victorian tribute to the Scottish hero and winner of the Battle of Stirling Bridge in 1297. Perched high on a rock called Abbey Craig, around which Wallace had camped before the battle, the Wallace Monument, with its fine bronze statue of William Wallace above the door, was opened in 1870.*

BELOW: *The Auld Brig (Old Bridge), a stone footbridge over the Forth river at Stirling. Romantically minded Victorian visitors to Stirling liked to think that this was the bridge that was at the centre of the battle won by William Wallace in 1297. In fact, Wallace's men probably fought at a wooden bridge, and this arched stone bridge was not built until about 1400.*

ABOVE: *The bridge over the Teith at Callander, with Ben Ledi in the background. The small burgh of Callander, at the junction of the rivers Teith and Lemy, was laid out mostly in the 18th century. In the 19th century it became a popular place from which to explore the Trossachs and Loch Katrine a few miles to the west.*

LEFT: *Callander, at the very start of the Highlands, offered Victorian fishermen plenty of sport in rivers well supplied with trout and salmon. The spire rising from the centre of the town is that of St Kessog's Church. Tradition has it that St Kessog was an Irish missionary who first preached the Word of God on the banks of the Teith in the 6th century.*

RIGHT: *Dunblane Cathedral, Dunblane, on Allan Water. The cathedral as it appears in this picture owed a great deal to sympathetic restoration begun late in the 19th century. Founded in a bishopric created by David I, most of Dunblane Cathedral was built in the 13th century. It was neglected after the Reformation, much of its roof fell in and the choir was used as a parish church for 300 years.*

BELOW: *Doune Castle, seen from the bridge over the River Teith. This castle, an outstanding example of 14th-century Scottish military/domestic architecture, was built on a main route north from Stirling into the Scottish Highlands. The castle came into the ownership of the earls of Moray, but by the end of the 18th century was a roofless ruin. In 1883, the 14th Earl of Moray began a careful programme of restoration which returned it to its former glory.*

ABOVE: *The High Street, Hawick. In the 19th century, this market town in the Borders turned itself into a knitting and weaving industry boom town. Knitting, based on the wool from local sheep, began as a cottage industry in the 18th century. Large mills for frame-knitting were built early in the 19th century and before long much of the world was wearing high quality knitwear and tweed from Hawick.*

RIGHT: *Abbotsford, seen from the Tweed. This splendid place was the home of Sir Walter Scott for 20 years. He bought a simple farmhouse near Melrose in 1811 and spent many years and much money converting it into a splendid Gothic pile. In his study at Abbotsford, Scott wrote many of his most famous novels, writing feverishly to help pay off the debts of his Edinburgh publishing house.*

CHAPTER ELEVEN

SOUTH-WEST SCOTLAND

As a quick turning of the pages that follow show, south-west Scotland in the 19th century was Burns Country – with one or two other names, including William Wallace, the earls of Moray and John Walker, having smaller roles in the history of the western side of the Scottish Lowlands. This was a mainly agricultural country of rolling hills and green river valleys. There were attractive little towns, many of them with associations with Scotland's finest lyric poet and most with the ruins of ancient castles nearby, and seaside resorts (with golf links attached) that grew in popularity as the century progressed.

ABOVE: *Ballantrae, on the coast road south of the Firth of Clyde, was not the setting for Robert Louis Stevenson's famous novel. Indeed, when the author visited here in 1876, some local people, misliking his eccentric clothes, threw stones at him.*

RIGHT: *Lincluden Abbey, on the outskirts of Dumfries. Lincluden was founded for Benedictine nuns in the 12th century and was made collegiate in the 14th. Within the creeper-covered remains were some of the finest 15th-century stonework in Scotland.*

LEFT: *The High Street, Dumfries. The large building in the centre of the picture, is Midsteeple, the town's former tolbooth and prison. The spire of Greyfriars Church, built in 1867 on the site of an ancient castle, rises behind. When the church was completed, a statue of Robert Burns, was set in front of it. During his five years as an excise officer in Dumfries, Burns wrote hundreds of poems and songs, including "Auld Lang Syne". He died in the town in 1796.*

BELOW: *The Town Hall, Annan. Annan was a busy shipping and shrimp fishing town on the Solway Firth. The Victorians built a viaduct across the Firth from Cumbria in 1869, to bring iron ore to this part of Scotland. It was only partly worth the effort, for the demand for iron ore dwindled and the viaduct, already weakened by a great storm and repaired, was closed after the First World War.*

ABOVE: *Annan, built on the lower reaches of the Annan river where it flowed into the Solway Firth. The town's hinterland included Annandale, one of three parallel river valleys that enclosed some of the loveliest scenery to be found in the Scottish Lowlands.*

OPPOSITE: *Market Day in Dumfries, the largest town in south-west Scotland. The waterfront wall above the River Nith offers a good perch for the cattlemen. Their cattle-drover ancestors in the 18th century drove their cattle for sale from here to Huntingdon in England. If they wished, the men here could read the distances to Huntingdon and other English market towns on the front of the Midsteeple in the High Street.*

RIGHT: *The 12th Earl of Eglinton built this fine mansion, Eglinton Castle, near Irvine on the Firth of Clyde early in the 19th century. The extravagant Eglinton Tournament, an attempt to revive the forms of medieval chivalry in 19th-century Scotland, was held in the country park around Eglinton Castle in 1839. The future Emperor Napoleon III was one of the "knights".*

ABOVE: *Drummon Castle: a castle built in the Scottish Tower-House (or Pele tower) style, set in a classically designed terraced garden.*

RIGHT: *Caerlaverock Castle, on the Solway Firth. This defensive stronghold of the Maxwells, later earls of Nithsdale, dates from the late 13th century, but was given a more elegant interior in the Italian Renaissance style in the 15th century. Covenanter rebels largely destroyed the castle in 1640, but enough remained of the beauty created by the Maxwells at Caerlaverock to impress later visitors.*

ABOVE: *The Cross marks the town centre of Kilmarnock. This busy town was famous in the 19th century for its association with two great names – Robert Burns and John Walker. Burns's first collection of poems,* Poems Chiefly in the Scottish Dialect, *was published in Kilmarnock in 1786. A quarter of a century later, John Walker, a Kilmarnock grocer, perfected a blend of whisky and began bottling it. By mid-century the Johnnie Walker blending and bottling plant at Kilmarnock was one of the biggest in the world.*

LEFT: *Irvine, on the Firth of Clyde. An ancient burgh and port, Irvine was where William Wallace's supporters deserted him and signed the Treaty of Irvine with the English in 1297. A much more attractive fact about the town is that the oldest surviving Burns Club in the world was established here in 1826. Burns had lived and worked in the town as a flax-dresser in 1781-2.*

LEFT: *Robert Burns, a passionate radical and Scotland's finest poet. This portrait is based on the only painting of Burns that was done from life. The artist Alexander Nasmyth painted it in 1787, when Burns was in Edinburgh. The painting became the most familiar image of Burns in the 19th century and was reproduced on the covers of books, on Mauchline-ware boxes, on tins of shortbread, on prints and postcards, and many other souvenirs of the poet.*

BELOW: *The national memorial to Robert Burns, the Burns Memorial Tower in Mauchline. The Tower was erected in 1896, the centenary of the poet's death. Burns was married to Jean Armour in Mauchline, and four of his children were buried in the churchyard.*

ABOVE: *The Grecian-style Burns Monument, a memorial to Robert Burns, erected near the Auld Brig o' Doon in Alloway in 1823. Robert Burns was born in Alloway, near Ayr, on 25 January 1759. Alloway's graceful arched bridge over the River Doon featured in Burns's lively poem about Tam o' Shanter and his encounter with witches in Alloway church.*

OPPOSITE: *The Burns Monument in Kilmarnock. This monument, which commemorates the fact that the poet's first work was published in Kilmarnock – earning him £20 and saving him from emigration to America – was erected in 1879. Relics of the poet were stored in the tower after it opened.*

CHAPTER TWELVE

CLYDESIDE

This most industrialized part of Scotland, spreading from either bank of the River Clyde and down its estuary to the Firth of Clyde, was dominated but not overpowered, by the great city of Glasgow. Centrally placed in the Clyde valley, with rich coalfields surrounding it and with deep-water docks stretching 20 miles up from the sea, it was not surprising that during the 19th century, Glasgow developed rapidly as one of the great cities of the post-Industrial Revolution age. Beyond the city lay a region of many towns of considerable historic interest and a land of great beauty, especially along the coasts of the Firth of Clyde and the great sea lochs that reached from it into the heart of the country, and all round glorious Loch Lomond, Scotland's largest loch.

ABOVE: *The new building for the University of Glasgow, opened in 1870. This vast Gothic edifice, designed by George Gilbert Scott, replaced the old buildings, dating back to the 17th century, where Adam Smith and James Watt had worked.*

RIGHT: *The seafront esplanade at Helensburgh, seen from the pier. This town, on Gare Loch on the Firth of Clyde, was an up-and-coming watering-place in the 1890s. The* Comet, *Europe's first steamboat, was launched on the Clyde here in 1812.*

LEFT: *Glasgow Cathedral, the only complete medieval cathedral on the Scottish mainland. Established in the 12th century, the cathedral was named after St Mungo, who had built a church in a place called Glasgu (meaning "beloved green place") in the 6th century. St Mungo's tomb, with its superb fan vaulting, survived in the crypt after much else was destroyed in the Reformation by anti-idolaters.*

LEFT: *Glasgow's elegant George Square, named after King George III, was designed and laid out in 1781. It quickly became the heart of the modern city, made prosperous by the Industrial Revolution and Victorian hard work. The pillar in the centre of the square was originally to have had a statue of George III on top. The honour eventually went to Sir Walter Scott.*

ABOVE: *Glasgow's great monument to the Railway Age, the solidly impressive St Enoch's Station. As with other important railway stations in the 19th century, St Enoch's Station incorporated a large, well-appointed hotel.*

ABOVE: *The tower and spire of George Gilbert Scott's Glasgow University reaches 300 feet (91 metres) above the Gothic-style university. The climb to the top was rewarding: splendid panoramic views of the city and surrounding countryside. Ready for occupancy in 1870, this imposing new structure gave Glasgow University the home that it had merited for centuries, given the quality of much of the work and research done in the old building in the High Street.*

RIGHT: *Glasgow Bridge over the Clyde in the centre of the city. This fine bridge, built by the Scottish engineer Thomas Telford in 1836, did not have much longer to last. It was replaced in 1899 by a much more massive structure.*

LEFT: *Teighness, in Arrochar, at the head of Loch Long. Arrochar's closeness to Loch Lomond, the largest and, for many, the loveliest loch in Scotland, just a couple of miles way, ensured the town a lively summer trade as a holiday centre.*

BELOW: *Trippers boarding paddle steamers at the landing-stage in Rothesay, the chief town of Bute, for a trip to the Kyles of Bute. Set on the edge of a sheltered bay, Rothesay had plenty of attractions for visitors. There was a fine esplanade, laid out with gardens and other amenities, the ruins of Rothesay Castle in the centre of town, and Mount Stewart, the seat of the Marquis of Bute, a few miles away.*

RIGHT: *The Kyles of Bute, the sounds lying between the island of Bute and the mainland peninsulas, seen from Bannatyne. This small town north of Rothesay was a port, with a landing stage used by steamers carrying holidaymakers around the sea loch-indented coast.*

ABOVE: *The pier at Dunoon, which had grown to become one of the larger watering places on the Clyde at the end of the 19th century. Castle Hill, above the main pier, had two, very different, points of interest for visitors. One was the remains of Dunoon Castle, once a stronghold of the Campbells. The other was a statue, set up in 1896, of Mary Campbell, Robert Burns's "Highland Mary", who was born in Dunoon.*

RIGHT: *Paddle steamers get ready to leave Princes Pier at Greenock, on the southern shore of the Firth of Clyde. Its position ensured that Greenock had long been a ship-building town. As the birthplace of James Watt, inventor of the condensing steam engine, Greenock could also lay claim to a place in the history of steam shipping.*

RIGHT: *East Bay, one of the two fine bays at Dunoon which had helped make the town a popular yachting and sailing centre. The Royal Clyde Yacht Club's house, at Hunter's Quay, was the headquarters for the spring regatta held every year off Dunoon.*

RIGHT: *The High Street in Dumbarton, a ship-building town on the north shore of the Firth of Clyde. Famous in legend as the place from which St Patrick was kidnapped and sold into slavery in Ireland and in history as the town from which the six-year-old Mary, Queen of Scots was sent to France, a more recent claim to fame was the fact that the Cutty Sark was built in the Dumbarton yard in 1869.*

RIGHT: *The mild air of Helensburgh, a charming town on Gare Loch, just 45 minutes by express train from Glasgow, ensured that any health establishments, such as the Shandon Hydropathic, pictured here, would win a good, regular clientele. The resort had a perfectly genteel history, too. It was built on the property of Sir James Colquhoun of Luss at the end of the 18th century and named after his wife, Helen.*

ABOVE: *A peaceful scene of reflections in calm waters at Strone, on the southerly point of the forest-covered land between Holy Loch and Loch Long. The buildings along the shoreline in the distance are at Hunter's Quay, in Dunoon.*

LEFT: *A quiet day in the main street at Largs, a popular resort and port. Ferry steamers made regular sailings from Largs to the nearby island of Great Cumbrae in the southern arm of the Firth of Clyde and to the many other islands in the Firth.*

LEFT: *Dunn Square, in Paisley. In the 19th century Paisley was famous for its beautiful, warm, distinctively patterned shawls, worn by every woman in the country, from Queen Victoria down, who could afford them. Shawl weaving began in Paisley in 1805. Weavers began copying the shawls that soldiers serving in Kashmir, in India, had been bringing home since the late 18th century. Although several places made the shawls, Paisley's were considered the best.*

ABOVE: *The seafront at Largs, seen from the pier. A sailing centre and a steamer port, Largs's most famous moment in history had happened seven centuries before. At the 1263 Battle of Largs, held at sea and, when a storm had driven the Norse galleys ashore, on land, the Scots, led by Alexander III, routed the forces of King Hakon of Norway. The famous battle ended the 400-year-old dominion of the Norsemen over the Hebrides and the Isle of Man.*

CHAPTER THIRTEEN

NORTHERN SCOTLAND

Samuel Johnson, visiting the Scottish Highlands in 1773, found a country of great beauty with an extraordinary power to move the mind and heart. Gazing upon the Cathedral and Abbey at Iona, he said, "That man is little to be envied…whose piety would not grow warmer upon Iona." In the next century, the Highlands continued to work their magic on all, including Queen Victoria herself, who were drawn to its many beautiful mountains, lochs and rivers, to ruined castles with ancient legends to tell, to blossoming new seaside resorts and handsome old towns and cities, and to the many islands of the Hebrides.

ABOVE: *Inveraray, on Loch Fyne. This "planned" village was built in the 18th century around a castle of the Campbells of Argyll. In 1745, the Campbells began rebuilding Inveraray Castle, which involved moving the town.*

RIGHT: *The ruins of Kilchurn Castle on Loch Awe in Glen Orchy. The once mighty castle was first built in about 1440 as the stronghold of the Campbells of Glenorchy, ancestors of the Campbells of Breadalbane.*

LEFT:
A paddle steamer moored at a jetty by the keep that was all that remained of Carrick Castle on Loch Goil. Another Campbell stronghold, Carrick Castle was built in the 14th and 15th centuries, possibly on the site of a Norse fort.

RIGHT:
Looking east across Loch Awe towards Ben Lui. Ruined Kilchurn Castle, on a spit of land jutting into Loch Awe, can be seen in the centre of the picture. The castle was lived in by the Campbells of Breadalbane until the mid-18th century. It was garrisoned by Hanoverian troops after the '45 Rising, and gradually fell into ruin afterwards. The top of one of its towers was blown off in a gale in 1879.

RIGHT:
Inveraray Castle, seat of the Campbells of Argyll, on Loch Fyne. A mansion rather than a fortification, the Castle was built between 1745 and 1790 to replace an older castle. In the second half of the 19th century, the castle became the Scottish home of Queen Victoria's daughter, Princess Louise, who married the 9th Duke of Argyll.

LEFT: *St Fillans, built at the outflow of the Earn river from Loch Earn in the Trossachs. South-east of the village was a ruined chapel, dating from the late 15th century, said to have been built on the site of cell in which the 8th-century saint, Fillan, had lived.*

LEFT: *The Cathedral on Iona. The tiny Inner Hebrides island, on which St Columba set foot in AD563, became the cradle of Christianity in Scotland and the burial place of 60 kings. Its beautiful cathedral, or abbey, dates mainly from the early 16th century, though there were many changes and additions in the centuries that followed. The cathedral was presented to the Church of Scotland by Iona's owner, the 8th Duke of Argyll, in 1899.*

LEFT: *Fingal's Cave on Staffa, an island in the Inner Hebrides. Known to very few outside the Hebrides until the explorer Sir Joseph Banks visited it in 1772, Staffa's extraordinary basalt formations, the result of volcanic activity, fascinated the 19th-century mind. Queen Victoria and Prince Albert, artists like J M W Turner, poets, including Scott, Wordsworth and Tennyson, and composers, most notably Mendelssohn, all made the sea journey to Staffa.*

ABOVE: *The town and harbour of Oban, considered by Victorians to be the capital of the Western Highlands, was the most important port serving the Western Isles. From the steamboat quay, steamers went to most of the Hebridean islands, providing many delightful excursions for visitors.*

LEFT: *Looking down on Inverness and the Ness river from the castle. The capital of the Highlands, recovered from the damage inflicted on it by both sides during the '45 Uprising, was a prosperous town in the 19th century. A new market in 1816 made it the centre of the Highlands wool and sheep trade, and the arrival of the railway in 1855 also helped it grow.*

LEFT: *Macduff, a small town on the Moray coast. This town in Banffshire, where the earls of Fife, chiefs of Clan Macduff, held much land, was a small place called Doune until 1783. Then the 2nd Earl of Fife decided to build a fishing village there, and gave it his family name, Macduff. In the 19th century, the village grew into an important fishing centre, with a harbour and a fish market.*

BELOW: *Banff, a seaport and resort at the mouth of the River Deveron on the Moray coast, sometimes called "the Scottish Riviera". The town's showpiece was Duff House, an imposing and palatial home of the earls, later dukes of Fife. Queen Victoria's grand-daughter, Princess Louise, married the Earl of Fife, later the 1st Duke of Fife. in 1884.*

OPPOSITE: *The cathedral (on the left) and castle at Inverness, seen from Ness Walk, along the bank of the Ness. The castle, built in the 1830s, replaced an older one blown up on the orders of Bonnie Prince Charlie. St Andrew's Cathedral, also a 19th-century structure, was given a richly decorated interior, in true Victorian style.*

ABOVE: *Ballater, on the River Dee, seen from Craigconach, a hill above the town. Ballater began life as a small spa, built by Francis Farquharson of Monaltrie, who had been spared hanging at the last minute after Culloden. His nephew turned the spa into a carefully planned town and summer centre early in the 19th century, and his plans were greatly helped by the arrival of the railway. The line from Aberdeen ended at Ballater, Queen Victoria having refused to allow it to come any closer, even though she frequently used it herself when travelling to Balmoral from Aberdeen.*

LEFT: *Balmoral Castle, on the River Dee in Aberdeenshire. Prince Albert bought a Scottish tower house here in 1852, partly because the country around it reminded him of his birthplace in Germany. He and Queen Victoria converted it with great enthusiasm into a beloved Highland home, moving in in 1855. Never happier than when she was at Balmoral, the Queen even published a book,* Leaves From The Journal of My Life in the Highlands, *about her life there – which allowed her Prime Minister, Disraeli, to talk about "we authors, Ma'am".*

LEFT: *The narrow 18th-century Brig o' Feugh, built over the River Feugh in its rugged gorge just before it joined the Dee, south of Banchory. In the 19th century, Banchory, which could trace its origins back to a 5th century saint, whose monastery was on the site of the town's church, was a summer holiday town. The fiddler and composer, James Scott Skinner, known as the "Strathspey King", was born in Banchory in 1843.*

ABOVE: *Castle Street in Aberdeen, Scotland's third largest and arguably most handsome city. In the 19th century, Aberdeen grew considerably. At the beginning of the century, ancient Castle Street was greatly extended by a new street, called Union Street in commemoration of the union of the parliaments of Britain and Ireland. This imposing street, built almost entirely of local granite, became Aberdeen's main east-west thoroughfare.*

BELOW: *A pleasant day on the banks of the broad River Tay, in Perth. An ancient city, once the capital of Scotland, Perth and its surroundings were among the loveliest country in the Highlands, much praised by writers and poets. Sir Walter Scott even wrote a novel,* The Fair Maid of Perth, *about the city. Perth's council made good use of the novel as a tourist attraction. A house on the site of the Fair Maid's house was restored in 1893, and scenes from the novel were included in the stained-glass windows of the City Chambers.*

BELOW: *The harbour at Stonehaven, a fishing port on the Mearns coast south of Aberdeen. This small town virtually became two towns in the 19th century, with Old Stonehaven clustered round the harbour and a new town being built on the hills above it. The inventor Robert William Thomson, who counted the pneumatic tyre and the fountain pen among his inventions, was born in Stonehaven in 1822.*

BELOW: *Wade's Bridge at Aberfeldy. This fine five-arched stone bridge over the River Tay, actually designed by William Adam, was built in 1733-35 by General George Wade. It was just one of many such bridges he built during the course of his work to put military roads through the Highlands, and thus bring the rebellious clan chiefs within the orbit of the government and its troops.*

RIGHT: *The Black Watch Monument, Aberfeldy. This cairn, surmounted by a kilted soldier, was erected near Wade's Bridge in 1887. It commemorates the incorporation of the Black Watch Regiment into the British Army in 1739. The regiment, which had been raised in the 1720s, got its name from the dark colours of the tartan in which its kilts were made.*

210

ABOVE: *Crieff, a pleasant market town on the way north from Stirling to Perth. Until the late 18th century, Crieff was one of the largest "trysts", or cattle markets, in Scotland. The loss of the cattle market to Stenhousemuir meant that Crieff had to turn to other ways to remain prosperous. Fortunately, the country around was well-supplied with attractions, from the beautiful Sma' Glen and Loch Earn to picturesque Drummond Castle.*

RIGHT: *The Bridge of Ross, at Comrie in the Trossachs. Because it is built right on the Highland Boundary Fault which divides the Lowlands of Scotland from the Highlands, Comrie sometimes shakes a bit – usually only enough to rattle crockery on shelves, but in 1839 strongly enough to crack house walls. This did not not prevent Comrie becoming a popular summer holiday town in the 19th century.*

CHAPTER FOURTEEN

LEINSTER

O ne of the four provinces into which Ireland was traditionally divided, Leinster roughly covered the south-east quarter of the island, although it stretched from well above the half-way line, taking in County Louth, down to the south-eastern tip of Ireland in Wexford, leaving three-quarters of the southern coastline to fall into the province of Munster. Most of Leinster lay around Dublin and included "the Pale", the area to which English control had shrunk by the beginning of the 16th century. The counties of Leinster, including Dublin, Wicklow and Kilkenny, contained within them areas of great natural beauty, towns of great historical significance, including Dublin and Kilkenny, resorts like Bray and Howth and, at Glendalough, one of the most important Christian sites in Ireland.

LEFT: *Glendalough, Co. Wicklow. One of the finest Round Towers in Ireland rises above one of its most atmospheric monastic sites. The 6th-century monastery, established by St Kevin, remained a place of pilgrimage, especially on St Kevin's feast day, 3 June.*

ABOVE: *College Green, at the heart of the city of Dublin. When Trinity College, the main entrance façade of which is at the centre of the picture, was founded by Elizabeth I in 1592, it was outside the walls of the city.*

ABOVE: *The harbour at Kingstown, on the south side of Dublin Bay. A fishing village in the early 19th century, Kingstown was given a splendid new harbour, to designs of John Rennie, and built between 1817 and 1859. The impressive harbour became the principal yacht station in Ireland, with the Kingstown Royal Harbour Boat Club occupying a handsome club house near the eastern pier. Kingstown itself was a pleasant and fashionable seaside resort.*

RIGHT: *Looking up Sackville Street from O'Connell Bridge, over the Liffey in Dublin. This generously wide bridge, opened in 1880, crossed the river from the old, artistic Temple Bar area of the city on the south bank to the busy commercial and shopping area on the north bank. It replaced the narrower Carlisle Bridge of 1794. The large statue in the centre of Sackville Street (re-named O'Connell Street in 1922) is of the politician Daniel O'Connell.*

RIGHT: *St Stephen's Green, Dublin, Originally an ancient common, the green was enclosed in the 17th century. It was laid out in the attractive style in the picture as recently as 1880. A generous grant from Lord Ardilaun, a member of the Guinness family, allowed for the creation of a lake and a fountain, set about with trees and flowerbeds, and with a bandstand and other amenities. The north side of the Green, called the Beaux' Walk, had several gentlemen's clubs on it.*

RIGHT: *A stone bridge arches over the River Dargle in County Wicklow. Flowing through the lovely Wicklow countryside, the Dargle was noted in guide books as one of the main attractions of the area, easily accessible from resorts like Bray.*

ABOVE: *The rocky islet in Dublin Bay called Ireland's Eye, seen from the hills above Howth. This fishing town at the northern limit of Dublin Bay was a popular resort with Dubliners. In the early 19th century Howth was the main Dublin harbour for packet and mail boats from England. But the harbour silted up and from 1833, Dun Laoghaire became Dublin's main port.*

RIGHT: *The elegant 19th-century formal gardens at Powerscourt, near Enniskerry in northern County Wicklow. An 18th-century mansion, Powerscourt was at the centre of a large estate set against the magnificent backdrop of the Great Sugar Loaf mountain. Within the vast estate was the Powerscourt Waterfall, where the River Dargle cascaded 425 feet (130 metres) over a granite escarpment.*

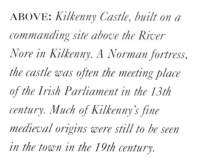

ABOVE: *Kilkenny Castle, built on a commanding site above the River Nore in Kilkenny. A Norman fortress, the castle was often the meeting place of the Irish Parliament in the 13th century. Much of Kilkenny's fine medieval origins were still to be seen in the town in the 19th century.*

LEFT: On the promenade at Bray, a resort in County Wicklow that developed after the railway was extended south from Dun Laoghaire in the 1850s. Guide books of the period waxed lyrical about Bray, calling it one of the most beautiful towns in Ireland. As one guide explained, "Its air is invigorating to a surprising degree, and the town is close to the grand scenery of the Wicklow Hills, one of the choicest districts in the Emerald Isle."

LEFT: On the promenade at Bray, a resort in County Wicklow that developed after the railway was extended south from Dun Laoghaire in the 1850s. Guide books of the period waxed lyrical about Bray, calling it one of the most beautiful towns in Ireland. As one guide explained, "Its air is invigorating to a surprising degree, and the town is close to the grand scenery of the Wicklow Hills, one of the choicest districts in the Emerald Isle."

BELOW: The Vale of Avoca, in the Wicklow Mountains. The poet, Thomas Moore, wrote of the beauty of this gentle and beautiful valley, ensuring that a drive to it would become a favourite excursion, culminating at the Meeting of the Waters, the confluence of the Avonbeg and Avonmore rivers.

CHAPTER FIFTEEN

MUNSTER

The south-western quarter of Ireland, in the province of Munster, included among its half dozen counties Cork and Kerry, two of the loveliest counties in all Ireland. From the middle of the 19th century this area saw a great increase in the numbers of people visiting for pleasure and to experience that up-lifting of the spirit that beautiful places and wild country where Nature, not Man, was in the ascendant could bestow. Unspoilt by later mass tourism, the Lakes of Killarney, which Queen Victoria visited twice, were indeed outstandingly beautiful. They also had a strong spiritual attraction, centred on places like the island of Innisfallen in Lough Leane. At Blarney Castle, the gift of eloquence could be tried for and at the Cliffs of Moher in County Clare the power of the sea experienced.

LEFT: *Its violent years far behind, Ross Castle, near Killarney in County Kerry, is the backdrop to a tranquil fishing scene. Built in the mid-15th century, Ross Castle was the last in Ireland to fall to Cromwell's forces in 1653.*

ABOVE: *Lisdoonvarna, County Clare. Well known for its mineral springs, this country town was also famous for its matchmakers who, for a fee, would match up young people looking for partners. The annual Match-making Festival took place in September.*

RIGHT: *Reginald's Tower, on the river quayside at Waterford, is one of the best-preserved parts of the city's fortifications. The Vikings were the first to build a settlement here, near the mouth of the River Suir. The city's walls and towers, begun by the Vikings, were strengthened and extended by the Anglo-Normans who, like the Vikings, recognized the strategic importance of the place.*

RIGHT: *The busy riverside quays at Waterford. Lying on the tidal reach of the River Suir, Waterford became in the 13th century the most powerful city in Ireland, protected by the favour of the kings of England. Because its port was the most important on Ireland's south coast, the town was also a big trading centre. Among the local industries that contributed to it's prosperity, glass-making, begun in the 18th century, was one of the most important. Just about every middle-class home in Victorian Britain and Ireland took pride in their collections of Waterford crystal and glass.*

ABOVE: *Cappoquin, a small market town set on hill overlooking the lovely plain of the Blackwater Valley in County Waterford. In 1832, a group of Irish monks founded an abbey a few miles to the north of Cappoquin. They had been expelled from the Cistercian abbey of Melleray in Brittany and named their new abbey in Ireland Mount Melleray.*

RIGHT: *Dunmore East, a picturesque little fishing town with many neat thatched cottages, set between chunky red sandstone cliffs near Waterford. The sailing craft mingling with the fishing boats signal that, at the end of the 19th century, the town was already popular as a holiday place for people from Waterford.*

ABOVE: *Queenstown, in County Cork, built on a magnificent harbour at the estuary of the River Lee. Originally called Cove, the port was renamed Queenstown after Queen Victoria arrived there on a State Visit in 1849. (After Independence, it was renamed Cobh.) A fine watering place, it was also a very busy commercial port, the first transatlantic steamer having sailed from Cove in 1838.*

ABOVE: *St Finbarr's Cathedral, in Cork, completed in 1878. In the 7th century, Saint Finbarr founded an abbey and school on marshy land round the mouth of the River Lee. The settlement that grew up around the abbey became the city of Cork. It is not surprising then, that when Cork was eventually given this fine cathedral in the Gothic Revival style, it was dedicated to the city's founder and patron saint.*

RIGHT: *Until 1800, St Patrick's Street, at the busy heart of Cork, was a waterway, with quays for large ships, and boats moored, Venice-style, at the steps of elegant, Georgian houses. Then in the early years of the 19th century, the water was diverted and the waterway paved over. The new street, called St Patrick's Street, soon became a main thoroughfare in the commercial and business heart of the city.*

LEFT: *Cromwell's Bridge, near Glengarriff. Throughout Ireland there are picturesque ruins that Cromwell's troops "knocked about a bit", to quote the music hall song. This bridge, overgrown with greenery, was one of them.*

RIGHT: *A tunnel through rocks at Glengarriff. This picture, clearly taken for what in the 20th century became the "tourism market", emphasizes the attractions of Glengarriff. Here are the Caha Mountains, through which a road had been blasted to Kenmare and the Lakes of Killarney in mid-century. And here, too, is a picturesque scene from Irish country life, with a white-aproned woman standing by the door of an old, turf-roofed cottage and watching a horse taking a well-earned drink.*

BELOW: *Glengarriff, in a sheltered position at the head of Bantry Bay in County Cork, was a favourite holiday place for well-off Victorians, drawn there by the mild climate and glorious scenery. Even Queen Victoria went there, sailing, like many of her subjects, from England to Ireland, then taking a train to Bantry and a paddle steamer from there to Glengarriff.*

LEFT: *Within the impressive ruins of the keep of 15th-century Blarney Castle lies what was, even in Victorian times, one of Ireland's big tourist attractions – the Blarney Stone. According to legend, kissing the Blarney Stone conferred on the kisser the gift of eloquence. In fact, Elizabeth I, exasperated with the contemporary Lord Blarney's ability to talk much while actually agreeing to do very little, started it. "It's all Blarney," she is supposed to have cried.*

ABOVE: *Bantry Bay, a turbulent stretch of water cutting a 30-mile (48-km) indent into the south-western tip of County Cork. Backed by the Beara Peninsula's dramatic Caha Mountains, the magnificently scenic bay provided numerous sheltered small bays and inlets for attractive resort towns like Bantry and Glengarriff.*

RIGHT: *The Lakes of Killarney, seen from the Kenmare road. With a road blasted through the Caha Mountains to Kenmare in mid-century, the Lakes of Killarney became accessible to every Victorian visitor with a love of magnificent lakes and superbly unspoilt mountain scenery.*

ABOVE: *The spectacular uplands of Macgillicuddy's Reeks, to the west of the Lakes of Killarney on the Iveragh peninsula in County Kerry. This region was one of the most visited in Ireland. Even Queen Victoria came to the Lakes of Killarney twice.*

BELOW: *The island of Innisfallen in Lough Leane, one of the three Killarney lakes. Innisfallen, the largest and loveliest of the many islands in Lough Leane, was an important centre of Irish scholarship for a thousand years after the first monastery was established there in the 7th century. The 11th-century High King, Brian Boru, was said to have been educated there and the magnificent* Annals of Innisfallen *was made there a century later.*

ABOVE: *The Gap of Dunloe, near the Lakes of Killarney. This dramatic glacier-carved mountain pass offered spectacular views in wild, virtually deserted country. Travellers hired a pony and trap for the drive up it. From about the mid-19th century they could stop for a drink at the southern end of the Gap at Kate Kearney's Cottage. Kate was a local beauty who ran an illegal drinking house in her cottage.*

LEFT: *The Old Weir Bridge on the Muckross Estate at the Lakes of Killarney was an extra attraction for visitors to the celebrated beauty spot, the Meeting of the Waters. This was the point at which the waters from the Upper Lake met Muckross Lake and Lough Leane.*

RIGHT: *Muckross Abbey, a Franciscan foundation dating from the mid-15th century. Muckross Abbey was suppressed by Henry VIII, but the monks returned and were still there when Cromwell's troops arrived, to turn them out and despoil the abbey. Its ruins were an oasis of calm and contemplation in the midst of the visitor attractions of the Lakes of Killarney.*

BELOW: *An unusually calm day by the Cliffs of Moher, in County Clare. Towering 600 feet (183 metres) at their highest point above the Atlantic Ocean, the Cliffs of Moher, spectacularly striated with bands of shale and sandstone, more often than not allowed visitors to experience the savage power of the sea as it beat against the rocks.*

CHAPTER SIXTEEN

CONNACHT

Ireland's historic province of Connacht (or Connaught), which included the counties of Galway, Mayo and Sligo, covered some of the wildest country in the west of Ireland. A sparsely populated land of windswept mountains and peat bogs, with a rugged Atlantic-facing coast, it was also a country rich in prehistoric sites and the remains of a vibrant monastic culture. The region suffered greatly during the Great Famine of the mid-19th century and emigration from Connacht was among the highest in Ireland. Places like Achill Island, Ireland's largest island, were left virtually deserted. Despite this, a rich Gaelic cultural tradition survived, much of it celebrated in the wonderful poetry of William Butler Yeats, a native of Sligo. As the Victorians discovered, there was a lot to enjoy in Connacht.

ABOVE: *Lough Gill, at the heart of Yeats country in County Sligo. The poet William Butler Yeats loved the county of his birth and spent as much time as possible there. Many of his poems were about the lake-studded landscape of Sligo.*

RIGHT: *Exploring a wind-and-sea-carved gap in the Minawn Cliffs on Achill Island in County Mayo. The largest of the islands off Ireland's coast, Achill Island was a very remote place in the 19th century.*

Clifden, the main town of Connemara in Galway. The town was a 19th-century creation, the work of a local landowner, John D'Arcy, who was the main force behind the establishment of Clifden in 1812. It never grew beyond a couple of main streets and a few side streets and alleys, but was still, at the end of the century, a convenient stopping place for visitors to Connemara.

ABOVE: *How the typical Irish colleen dressed: a pretty girl posing in traditional shawl, head-covering and neat white apron. This was the Victorian tourism image of Irish women.*

RIGHT: *An Irishwoman at her spinning wheel. The spinning and weaving of woollen cloth was an important money-earning craft for many in the west of Ireland throughout the 19th century.*

RIGHT: *This late Victorian postcard of Galway sums up the Ireland of the tourist industry – all bunches of shamrock, jaunting cars, lovely Irish colleens and sturdy Irish peasants. It was reality sanitized, prettified and made as attractive as possible.*

IRISH PEASANT

THE · IRISH JAUNTING OR "OUTSIDE CAR."

IRISH PEASANT GIRL.

ABOVE: *Looking up Killary Bay (now called Killary Harbour) towards Mweelrea Mountain, in Connemara, County Galway. Killary Bay, Ireland's only fiord, was deep, dark and cold and led into some very wild, boggy and barren country. But there were also fine loughs and rivers, ideal for a day's fishing.*

LEFT: *Ballynahinch Lake, in the south of County Galway. It was one of many small lakes whose glinting waters broke the surface of the boggy plain that led from the coast at Roundstone and Errisbeg to the Connemara mountain ranges in the north. The splendid Ballynahinch Castle here was later owned by a maharajah and then became a hotel.*

BELOW: *Achill Head, where Achill Island plunges into the Atlantic Ocean. A clifftop walk here, along cliffs said to be the highest in Europe, was an exhilarating experience for the few visitors to the island in the 19th century. The island's only real village in the 19th century was Slievemore, where the owners of summer grazing cattle had their "booley houses". These were abandoned sometime in the mid-19th-century, probably because their owners had been driven away by the Great Famine.*

CHAPTER SEVENTEEN

ULSTER

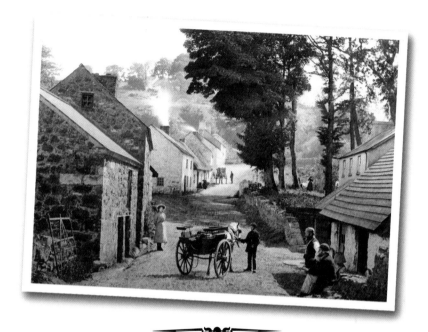

The ancient kingdom of Ulster was made up of nine counties, many of which had been kingdoms and chiefdoms in their own right, clustered at the top of the island of Ireland. St Patrick landed in Ireland in County Down in 432, and it was in Ulster that Christianity first replaced the old Celtic beliefs in Ireland. There were also strong links between Ulster and Scotland, close enough to the north coast of Antrim, legend had it, for the great warrior Finn MacCool to be able to step across the sea by way of a causeway of basalt columns he threw out from the coast. The Industrial Revolution influenced Ulster more than any other part of Ireland, with Belfast growing during the 19th century into one of the world's major ship-building cities. For Victorians, including the Queen, Ulster's greatest glories lay outside Belfast, in the magnificent scenery of coasts and inland lakes.

LEFT: *Glencoe in the Glens of Antrim. The Glens of Antrim, nine beautiful valleys carved by rivers through the wild, remote country inland from the coast of Antrim, became accessible to travellers when a coast road was built in 1834.*

ABOVE: *Woodside, Rostrevor, County Down. The Victorians turned Rostrevor, on the eastern shore of Carlingford Lough with the lovely Mountains of Mourne as a backdrop, into an attractive resort, called by guide books the "Montpellier of Ireland".*

RIGHT: *Cave Hill, its "Napoleon's Nose" profile clearly outlined against the sky, rises up beyond the northern edge of the city of Belfast. From the top of Cave Hill, where Wolfe Tone and leaders of the United Irishmen pledged themselves to rebellion in 1795, Belfast's citizens a hundred years later could easily see how greatly their city had grown in their lifetime. They could see most of Belfast and its busy shipyards and, on a clear day, parts of Scotland, too.*

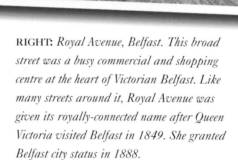

BELOW: *The Albert Memorial Clock Tower in Belfast was erected in 1867 in memory of the Prince Consort, who died in 1861. Although the Prince had no personal connections with the city, the memorial to him soon became one of its best-known landmarks; there is no sign here of the tilt, caused by subsidence, that would increase interest in it for later generations.*

RIGHT: *Royal Avenue, Belfast. This broad street was a busy commercial and shopping centre at the heart of Victorian Belfast. Like many streets around it, Royal Avenue was given its royally-connected name after Queen Victoria visited Belfast in 1849. She granted Belfast city status in 1888.*

LEFT: *The ruins of Dunluce Castle dominate a steep crag of the Causeway Coast of County Antrim, much as the original fortress castle had done since the 14th century. Long abandoned by its most prominent owners, the Scottish MacDonnell clan, Lords of the Isles and chiefs of Antrim, Dunluce Castle in the 19th century still retained within its walls enough reminders of its past glories to fascinate visitors.*

BELOW: *Portrush, on the Causeway Coast of County Antrim, grew in Victorian times into an attractive seaside resort which guide books, ignoring the claims of nearby Portstewart, referred to as the chief watering-place of the north of Ireland. Apart from its fine, smooth sands, Portrush's greatest attractions in the late 19th century were its golf links and its electric tramway link to the Giant's Causeway, a few miles away.*

ABOVE: *The Carrick-a-rede rope bridge, on Antrim's Causeway Coast, was almost as popular an attraction for Victorians as the natural wonder of the Giant's Causeway, further along the coast. The bridge, rebuilt every year by fishermen, made a precarious link from the coastal cliffs to Carrick-a-rede Island, where there were fisheries well worth the effort put into getting there.*

245

ABOVE: *Glenariff, considered by most Victorian visitors to be the loveliest of the nine Glens of Antrim. A wide and lush valley, Glenariff's greatest attraction was a spectacular series of waterfalls in a steep gorge, round whose sheer sides Victorian ingenuity and know-how had built a timber walkway.*

RIGHT: *The Honeycomb Rocks of the Giant's Causeway, County Antrim. Almost from 1693, when the Royal Geographical Society in London pronounced it to be one of the greatest wonders of the natural world, the Giant's Causeway was a major tourist attraction. Most Victorians were very impressed by the polygonal basalt rock formations; a few, like the author William Makepeace Thackeray, visiting in 1842, were put off by the money-making activities of armies of "guides".*

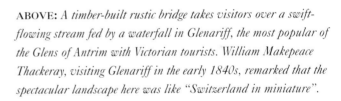

ABOVE: *A timber-built rustic bridge takes visitors over a swift-flowing stream fed by a waterfall in Glenariff, the most popular of the Glens of Antrim with Victorian tourists. William Makepeace Thackeray, visiting Glenariff in the early 1840s, remarked that the spectacular landscape here was like "Switzerland in miniature".*

LEFT: *Londonderry, in a fine setting along the River Foyle, was the second city of Ulster in the 19th century. The old town of Derry, site of a monastery founded by St Columba in the 6th century, got its "London" prefix in 1613 when it was chosen as the place for one of James VI and I's biggest Plantations in Ireland, the organizers being London livery companies. Although Londonderry was the official name of both town and its county, most people continued to refer to both as "Derry".*

RIGHT: *The Temple Arch at Horn Head, on the wild, west-facing Atlantic coast of County Donegal. An impressive quartzite rock face towering over 600 feet (183 metres) and including steep, ledged cliffs, caves and sea-stacks, Horn Head was doubly attractive to Victorians. The scenery was spectacular and the cliffs provided nesting sites for countless numbers of birds, including puffins, gulls and guillemots.*

BELOW: *The well-preserved ruins of Donegal Castle, in the town of Donegal, present their Jacobean face to the world. Early in the 17th century, Sir Basil Brooke took the 15th-century castle in hand, transforming it from a dour fortification into a combination of castle and attractive domestic dwelling, with mullions, gables and arches – and 14 fireplaces.*

RIGHT: *Killybegs, on Killibegs Bay in the south of Donegal, was popular with Victorian tourists. They liked its clean, pleasant seaport atmosphere and the fact that the "charming little place" made the perfect starting point for excursions to Carrick and Slieve League, whose "gigantic mass" was not difficult to ascend and from which the views were stupendous.*

LEFT: *Lower Lough Erne, County Fermanagh. Rich in prehistoric and medieval Christian sites, Lower Lough Erne and the country around it attracted Victorian visitors because of its history, its lovely scenery – and the superb angling available in the lough.*

BELOW: *Enjoying the quiet air of the Esplanade at Warrenpoint, at the head of Carlingford Lough in County Down. A thriving market town, Warrenpoint was also a popular resort with a first-rate bathing beach. Visitors came to Warrenpoint by train, tram and coach from nearby towns and by steam packet sailings twice a week from Liverpool.*

RIGHT: *The ruins of the most important of the monasteries around Lower Lough Erne, on Devenish Island. St Molaise founded a monastery on Devenish Island in the 6th century. Surviving Viking raids and fire, the monastery was still an important religious centre in the 17th century. Its 12th-century round tower survived virtually unscathed much longer, as this picture shows.*

LEFT: *Looking down Carlingford Lough towards its entrance from the sea. Dominating the land on the eastern, Ulster side of the lough, are the Mountains of Mourne which, to quote the 19th-century composer, Percy French, "sweep down to the sea". Never easy of access, the Mountains of Mourne were viewed by many Victorian visitors on comfortable excursions from such Carlingford Lough towns as Rostrevor and Warrenpoint.*

Italicized figures indicate illustrations